HOUGHTON MIFFLIN

Reading

Diagnostic Assessment
Grades 1–6

HOUGHTON MIFFLIN

ILLUSTRATION
Ruth Flanigan; Eileen Hine

ACKNOWLEDGMENTS
Houghton Mifflin Diagnostic Assessment is based on the "CORE Phonics Survey" pages 63–80 from *CORE Assessing Reading: Multiple Measures for Kindergarten Through Eighth Grade*, Arena Press, Novato, CA. Copyright © 1999 by Consortium On Reading Excellence, Inc. Reprinted by permission of Consortium On Reading Excellence, Inc.

For each of the selections listed below, grateful acknowledgment is made for permission to excerpt and/ or reprint original or copyrighted materials, as follows:

Selection from *A Chair for My Mother*, by Vera B. Williams. Copyright © 1982 by Vera B. Williams. Reprinted by permission of Greenwillow Books, a division of HarperCollins Publishers.

Selection from *An Octopus Is Amazing*, by Patricia Lauber. Copyright © 1990 by Patricia Lauber. Reprinted by permission of HarperCollins Publishers.

Selection from *The Midnight Fox*, by Betsy Byars. Copyright © 1968 by Betsy Byars. Reprinted by permission of Viking Penguin, a Division of Penguin Young Readers Group, a Member of Penguin Group (USA) Inc., 345 Hudson Street, New York, NY I0014. All rights reserved.

Selection from *Tornado Alert*, by Franklyn M. Branley. Copyright © 1988 by Franklyn M. Branley. Reprinted by permission of HarperCollins Publishers.

Selection from *All for the Better*, by Nicholasa Mohr. Copyright © 1992 by Sopris West Educational Services. Reprinted by permission of Sopris West.

Selection from *Rattlesnakes*, by Russell Freedman. Copyright © 1986 by Russell Freedman. Reprinted by permission of the author.

Selection from "The Girl Who Cried Flowers," from *The Girl Who Cried Flowers and Other Tales*, by Jane Yolen. Copyright © 1974 by Jane Yolen. Reprinted by permission of Curtis Brown, Ltd.

Selection from *The Great Yellowstone Fire*, by Carole Garbuny Vogel and Kathryn Allen Goldner. Copyright © 1990 by Carole Garbuny Vogel and Kathryn Allen Goldner. Published by Sierra Club Books/ Little, Brown and Company. Reprinted by permission of McIntosh & Otis, Inc.

Printed in the U.S.A.

ISBN: 978-0-547-15396-4

4 5 6 7 8 9 1409 17 16 15 14 13 12 11 10

Overview of *Diagnostic Assessment*

The *Diagnostic Assessment* provides information on a student's performance on the essential skills and strategies necessary to be a successful reader. The test can be administered by classroom teachers or reading specialists.

For students who have low scores on a group-administered test, the individually administered *Diagnostic Assessment* helps identify the specific areas where students show limited development and would benefit from focused instruction. Different sections of the test show how students apply skills to isolated words *and* to reading passages. The results of the test provide a baseline of student performance. (Note: For students who have difficulty with the phonemic awareness tasks and are at the emerging stages of literacy, use the *Emerging Literacy Survey*.)

There are two sections to *Diagnostic Assessment*. The first examines Phonemic Awareness and Phonics/Decoding. The second examines a student's skills and strategies in decoding, fluency, and comprehension while reading passages aloud.

SECTION ONE

Phonemic Awareness Phonemic awareness is the ability to hear and manipulate sounds in words. It is the understanding that spoken words are a collection of sounds. It is an auditory skill and does not rely on print. Phonemic awareness is a strong predictor of success with phonics and decoding. This test assesses three key phonemic awareness skills that directly support beginning decoding (beginning sounds, phoneme blending, phoneme segmentation).

Phonics/Decoding Phonics and decoding are print-based skills. Students learn to recognize that letters stand for sounds and those sounds are put together to form words. In this *Diagnostic Assessment*, students are asked to decode words with a range of phonic elements that progress in difficulty.

To assess a student's strategies with sounds and decoding accurately, it is important to look at the results of all of the subtests. By reviewing a student's errors as a whole, patterns emerge and instruction can be targeted to the needs of the student.

SECTION TWO

Section two of *Diagnostic Assessment* contains reading passages that are sequenced from beginning first grade through a beginning sixth grade reading level.

Each student reads selected passages aloud while you note errors. Then, the student is asked to retell the content of the passage and orally answer comprehension questions. As a result, the passages allow you to focus on a student's skills and strategies in *decoding, fluency,* and *comprehension*. Keeping in mind the decoding strengths and weaknesses identified in Section One, you can observe how the student applies those skills and strategies in running text as the passages are read orally.

The passages represent a variety of story types and interests, with a narrative and an expository selection at each grade. The content is developmentally appropriate, and the passages are designed for easy administration and scoring. The test results allow you to assess whether the student reads at, below, or above grade level.

Decoding Accuracy A decoding accuracy score gives you the percentage of words that the student reads correctly. After analyzing all errors, you can determine the areas that need more specific instruction. For example, a student may consistently miss words with consonant digraphs or vowel diphthongs.

Fluency Within Section Two there are two ways to evaluate fluency, which is defined as *reading rate* plus attention to *phrasing and expression*. The reading rate is assessed by calculating words correct per minute, or WCPM. Phrasing and expression, which reflect a student's understanding of the text, are scored by using a 4-point rubric that is provided for you.

Comprehension Comprehension is assessed using two different measures. First, the student reads the passage and then retells it in his or her own words. The value of retelling is in determining the student's understanding of the important concepts of the passage. The student should be able to tell the main idea and most important details, keeping the ideas in logical sequence. After the retelling, the student answers comprehension questions. It is especially important to note the *types* of questions that pose difficulty for the student, such ones that involve literal thinking, inferences, or vocabulary.

Taken together, the scores from Section One and Section Two give you a comprehensive picture of the student's strengths and weaknesses to guide instruction.

SECTION ONE:

Phonemic Awareness and Phonics/Decoding Skills

Administering and Scoring

SECTION ONE

What is the *Phonemic Awareness and Phonics/Decoding Skills* section?

Section One of *Diagnostic Assessment* test evaluates the phonemic awareness and phonics/decoding skills that have a high rate of application in beginning decoding. Each task presents a number of items, and the student manipulates sounds, identifies letters, or decodes words. Pseudowords, or made-up words, are included since the student must use decoding skills to correctly pronounce them and cannot have memorized them.

These assessments are best used to plan instruction for students who lack basic decoding skills and to develop instructional groups. They may be administered after instruction to assess progress.

Section Two of this test addresses a student's reading ability in the areas of comprehension, fluency, and decoding while reading connected text. Further information on administering and scoring this portion of test begins on page 28.

Why administer this section of *Diagnostic Assessment?*

A student's ability to use knowledge of sound/letter correspondences (phonics) to decode words determines, in large measure, his or her ability to read individual words. A detailed assessment of a student's phonics skills points to areas in which the student is likely to benefit most from systematic, explicit phonics instruction. In addition, knowing the skills that the student does possess will help in selecting reading tasks that offer the most effective reinforcement of those skills.

How do I administer the tests, and how long will it take?

It is usually best to choose among the subtests, based on a student's recent performance. First, estimate the student's general reading level, using any information you already have. Begin testing with the tasks designated for that level, according to the chart below. For example, for a fourth-grade student estimated to be reading at a second-grade level, you might begin with tasks for Early-mid Grade 2. Move to the next higher or lower tasks, based on whether the performance meets the benchmarks.

- Individually administered tests
- 15–25 minutes of testing time
- Administer the tasks appropriate to the student's performance level:

Beginning of Grade 1	Tasks 1–8A
Mid-late Grade 1	Tasks 1–8E, 9A
Early-mid Grade 2	Tasks 1–8G, 9A, 9B
Mid-late Grade 2	Tasks 7–8H, 9A, 9B
Grades 3–6	Tasks: 8–9C

What materials do I need to administer Section One?

- **Recording Forms** (See pages 14–21.) Duplicate one copy for each student. Permission is granted for reproduction of these pages.
- **Student Copy Blackline Masters** (See Masters 11–14, pages 22–25.) Duplicate one set and mount each page on card stock or a folder for durability, if desired. Permission is granted for reproducing these pages.
- Lined paper and pencil for each student
- One blank sheet of paper

What procedures do I use to administer the test?

Using any information you already have, choose where to begin testing. For example, if an older student is already decoding one-syllable words, accurately, you may omit the tasks for phonemic awareness and letter names/sounds.

Instructions for administering each of the tasks in Section One are included on the Recording Forms. Students read from the Student Copy. To focus the student's attention on the part of the test that is being given, cover the other parts with a piece of paper. The Recording Form shows the same material that appears on the Student Copy, but it is arranged so that you may easily record the student's responses.

Directions for administering **Section Two: Text Reading** begin on page 28.

How do I score Section One?

After administering Section One, transfer the student's scores to the Phonemic Awareness and Phonics/Decoding Test Summary Form. Use the next section to analyze the results for each student and plan instruction.

How do I analyze Section One?

Use the following guidelines to analyze each student's performance and plan instruction.

1. Use the Scoring and Analysis Summary (pages 12–13) to tally the student's scores and make notes about patterns of errors.

2. Carefully review the sample case study on pages 8–11 to help you learn to use this process.

3. Locate your student's pattern of phonemic awareness and phonics/decoding behaviors in the chart on pages 6–7. Use the suggestions provided to plan instruction. Record your plans on the Scoring and Analysis Summary (pages 12–13).

Using the Results

Grade	Benchmark performance = 80% on these tasks	If student scores less than 80% on these tasks …	Provide instruction in these skills …
Early Grade 1	Tasks 1–7, 8A	Task 1 Task 2 Task 3	Beginning Sounds Phoneme Blending Phoneme Segmentation
		Tasks 4–7	Letter Names and Sounds
		Task 8	Reading CVC words
Mid-late Grade 1	Tasks 1–7, 8A–E, 9A	Task 1 Task 2 Task 3	Beginning Sounds Phoneme Blending Phoneme Segmentation
		Tasks 4–7	Letter Names and Sounds
		Tasks 8A–E, 9A	Decoding and Spelling (specific phonic elements)
Early-mid Grade 2	Tasks 1–8G, 9A–B	Tasks 1–7	Beginning Sounds Phoneme Blending Phoneme Segmentation Letter Names and Sounds
		Tasks 8A–F, 9A–B	Decoding and Spelling (specific phonic elements)
		Task 8G	Two-syllable Words

Grade	Benchmark performance = 80% on these tasks	If student scores less than 80% on these tasks …	Provide instruction in these skills …
Mid-late Grade 2	Tasks 7–8A–H, 9A–C	Task 7	Vowel Sounds
		Task 8A–F, 9A–C	Decoding and Spelling (specific phonic elements)
		Tasks 8G–H	Multisyllabic Words
Grades 3–6	Tasks 8A–H, 9A–C	Task 8A–F, 9A–C	Decoding and Spelling (specific phonic elements)
		Task 8G–H	Multisyllabic Words

Sample Case Study: Mark Lester

Name *Mark Lester*   Date 11/20   **Diagnostic Assessment** SECTION ONE

Houghton Mifflin
Diagnostic Assessment

Scoring and Analysis Summary

Name   Grade   Date

Phonemic Awareness and Phonics/Decoding Summary Sheet

Phonemic Awareness Skills   **Observations**

___/8	(6)	Task 1.	Beginning Sounds
___/8	(6)	Task 2.	Phoneme Blending
___/8	(6)	Task 3.	Phoneme Segmentation

Because Mark's estimated reading level is Grade 3, I started testing with Task 8. He met benchmarks, so no need to go back to Tasks 1–7.

Alphabet Skills

___/26	(21)	Task 4.	Letter names—uppercase
___/26	(21)	Task 5.	Letter names—lowercase
___/23	(18)	Task 6.	Consonant sounds
___/5	(4)	Task 7.	Long-vowel sounds
___/5	(4)		Short-vowel sounds

Task 8: Reading and Decoding Skills

10/10	(8)	A.	Short vowels in CVC words
9/10	(8)	B.	Short vowels, digraphs, and -tch trigraph
20/20	(16)	C.	Short vowels and consonant blends
10/10	(8)	D.	Long vowels
10/10	(8)	E.	*r*- and *l*-controlled vowels
10/10	(8)	F.	Vowel diphthongs

Gave /p/ for ph in pseudoword. (probably not a problem, will review)

Can apply basic decoding to one-syllable words.

Multisyllabic Words:

24/24	(19)	G.	Two-syllable words
3/8	(6)	H.	Multisyllabic words

Has trouble decoding multisyllabic words.

Scoring and Analysis Summary, page 2

Name _____ Grade _____ Date _____

Task 9: Spelling Skills   Observations

_5_/5 (4)   A. Initial consonants

_5_/5 (4)   B. Final consonants

_5_/5 (4)   C. Short-vowel word

_5_/5 (4)   D. Long-vowel word

Instructional Needs

Skills to review: _Quick review of ph = /f/_ _____

_____

_____

_____

_____

Skills to teach: _Focus on application of all decoding skills to multisyllabic words._
Emphasize lessons on decoding longer words.
Reteach lessons and provide extra support as needed during
small-group instruction.
Check decoding progress regularly.

Note: *Numbers within parentheses show benchmarks for on-level performance.*

Phonemic Awareness, Phonics/Decoding   13   Scoring and Analysis Summary 2
Copyright © Houghton Mifflin Company. All rights reserved.   Blackline Master 2

Directions

Study the Scoring and Analysis Summaries and comments on Mark Lester to help you learn to analyze Section One, Phonemic Awareness and Phonics/Decoding Skills.

Background on Mark Lester

- Eleven-year-old fifth grader
- Reading approximately third-grade level

Analysis and Discussion

- Mark missed the *ph* digraph. This is probably not a problem but may require review.
- Mark applies basic decoding skills to one-syllable words but has difficulty applying skills to multisyllabic words.
- Mark uses basic decoding skills to spell words.
- Mark's difficulty in applying skills to multisyllabic words is likely to be affecting his fluency; that should be assessed with Text Reading passages in Section Two. Such a lack of fluency would likely have a negative effect on comprehension, which would account for Mark's low comprehension score on standardized achievement tests.
- Mark's major need is to learn to apply decoding skills to multisyllabic words. Check to make sure Mark understands lessons on decoding longer words, and reteach lessons for those skills as needed. Mark may also benefit from additional instruction and support during small-group lessons. His progress in decoding should be checked regularly.

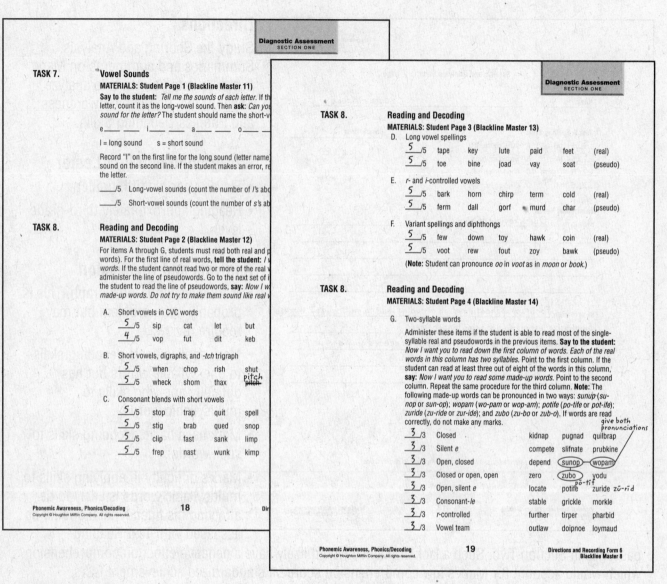

Diagnostic Assessment
SECTION ONE

TASK 7. **Vowel Sounds**

MATERIALS: Student Page 1 (Blackline Master 11)

Say to the student: *Tell me the sounds of each letter. If th____*
letter, count it as the long-vowel sound. Then **ask:** *Can yo____*
sound for the letter? The student should name the short-v____

e ___ ___   i ___ ___   a ___ ___   o ___ ___

l = long sound   s = short sound

Record "l" on the first line for the long sound (letter name____
sound on the second line. If the student makes an error, re____
the letter.

___/5   Long-vowel sounds (count the number of *l*'s abo____

___/5   Short-vowel sounds (count the number of *s*'s ab____

TASK 8. **Reading and Decoding**

MATERIALS: Student Page 2 (Blackline Master 12)

For items A through G, students must read both real and p____
words). For the first line of real words, **tell the student:** *I* ____
words. If the student cannot read two or more of the real v____
administer the line of pseudowords. Go to the next set of i____
the student to read the line of pseudowords, **say:** *Now I w____*
made-up words. Do not try to make them sound like real ____

A. Short vowels in CVC words

5/5	sip	cat	let	but
4/5	vop	fut	dit	keb

B. Short vowels, digraphs, and -tch trigraph

5/5	when	chop	rish	shut
5/5	wheck	shom	thax	~~pitch~~ *pitch*

C. Consonant blends with short vowels

5/5	stop	trap	quit	spell
5/5	stig	brab	qued	snop
5/5	clip	fast	sank	limp
5/5	frep	nast	wunk	kimp

TASK 8. **Reading and Decoding**

MATERIALS: Student Page 3 (Blackline Master 13)

D. Long vowel spellings

5/5	tape	key	lute	paid	feet	(real)
5/5	toe	bine	joad	vay	soat	(pseudo)

E. *r*- and *i*-controlled vowels

5/5	bark	horn	chirp	term	cold	(real)
5/5	ferm	dall	gorf	murd	char	(pseudo)

F. Variant spellings and diphthongs

5/5	few	down	toy	hawk	coin	(real)
5/5	voot	rew	fout	zoy	bawk	(pseudo)

(**Note:** Student can pronounce *oo* in *voot* as in *moon* or *book*.)

TASK 8. **Reading and Decoding**

MATERIALS: Student Page 4 (Blackline Master 14)

G. Two-syllable words

Administer these items if the student is able to read most of the single-syllable real and pseudowords in the previous items. **Say to the student:** *Now I want you to read down the first column of words. Each of the real words in this column has two syllables.* Point to the first column. If the student can read at least three out of eight of the words in this column, **say:** *Now I want you to read some made-up words.* Point to the second column. Repeat the same procedure for the third column. **Note:** The following made-up words can be pronounced in two ways: *sunup* (*su-nop* or *sun-op*); *wopam* (*wo-pam* or *wop-am*); *potife* (*po-tife* or *pot-ife*); *zuride* (*zu-ride* or *zur-ide*); and *zubo* (*zu-bo* or *zub-o*). If words are read correctly, do not make any marks.

give both pronunciations

3/3	Closed	kidnap	pugnad	quilbrap
3/3	Silent *e*	compete	slifnate	prubkine
3/3	Open, closed	depend	(sunop)	(wopam)
3/3	Closed or open, open	zero	(zubo)	yodu
3/3	Open, silent *e*	locate	potife *po-tif*	zuride *zŭ-rĭd*
3/3	Consonant-*le*	stable	grickle	morkle
3/3	*r*-controlled	further	tirper	pharbid
3/3	Vowel team	outlaw	doipnoe	loymaud

Points to note

• Mark has no real problems with short vowels, most digraphs, and consonant blends.

Analysis and Comments

• On Task 8B, Mark was unable to give the correct sound for the *ph* digraph in a pseudoword. This information is the basis for a quick review of this skill.

TASK 8. **Reading and Decoding**

MATERIALS: Student Page 4 (Blackline Master 14)

H.   Multisyllabic Words

Administer these items only if the student is able to read six of the items in Task 8G, column 1. **Say to the student:** *Now I want you* *down the first column of words. Each of the real words in this* *has more than two syllables.* Point to the first column. If the st* read at least three of the four words in this column, **say:** *Now* *to read some made-up words.* Point to the second column. If t are read correctly, make no marks. If words are read incorrect the student's response above the word. Expected pronunciatio pseudowords are given below the word.

1/2   (Closed, unaccented, closed)   caravan   petin
(pet
(pe t

0/2   (*r*-controlled, unaccented, silent *e*)   marmalade   dorli
(dor

1/2   (Open, closed, closed)   momentum   bolar
(bo l
(bol

1/2   (Closed, unaccented, vowel team)   velveteen   matl
(mat
(mat

TASK 9.   **Spelling**

A.   Give the student a pencil and a sheet of lined paper. **Tell the student:** *Number your paper from 1 through 5. Listen to each of the words I* *read and write the first sound you hear.* Write the student's responses over the words.

5/5   1. fit   2. map   3. pen   4. kid   5. hand

B.   **Tell the student:** *Number 1 through 5. Listen to each of the words I read, and write the first sound you hear.*

5/5   1. rub   2. fled   3. leg   4. sell   5. less

C.   **Tell the student:** *Number 1 through 10. Listen to each of the words I read, and write the whole word.*

1. fork	6. coin
2. yarn	7. float
3. sip	8. steep
4. shop	9. drive
5. tub	10. spoon
5/5	5/5

Points to Note

• The tasks on these pages involve both reading and spelling.

Analysis and Comments

• Mark is able to apply basic decoding skills to one- and two-syllable words. When he gives both pronunciations for pseudowords, this shows that he has good understanding of decoding strategies and the applications of phonics.

• Mark does not appear to know how to apply the decoding skills he uses in one- and two-syllable words to longer words. This supports the decision to emphasize Decoding Longer Words lessons.

• As far as spelling is concerned, Mark is able to use basic decoding skills of beginning consonants, ending consonants, short medial vowels, long vowels, *r*-controlled vowels, and vowel diphthongs to spell one-syllable words.

Houghton Mifflin
Diagnostic Assessment

Scoring and Analysis Summary

Name   **Grade**   **Date**

Phonemic Awareness and Phonics/Decoding Summary Sheet

Phonemic Awareness Skills   **Observations**

_____/8   (6)   Task 1.   Beginning Sounds

_____/8   (6)   Task 2.   Phoneme Blending

_____/8   (6)   Task 3.   Phoneme Segmentation

Alphabet Skills

_____/26   (21)   Task 4.   Letter names—uppercase

_____/26   (21)   Task 5.   Letter names—lowercase

_____/23   (18)   Task 6.   Consonant sounds

_____/5   (4)   Task 7.   Long-vowel sounds

_____/5   (4)   Short-vowel sounds

Task 8: Reading and Decoding Skills

_____/10   (8)   A.   Short vowels in CVC words

_____/10   (8)   B.   Short vowels, digraphs,
                        and -tch trigraph

_____/20   (16)   C.   Short vowels and
                        consonant blends

_____/10   (8)   D.   Long vowels

_____/10   (8)   E.   *r*- and *l*-controlled vowels

_____/10   (8)   F.   Vowel diphthongs

Multisyllabic Words:

_____/24   (19)   G.   Two-syllable words

_____/8   (6)   H.   Multisyllabic words

Scoring and Analysis Summary, page 2

Name _____ **Grade** _____ **Date** _____

Task 9: Spelling Skills   **Observations**
_____

____/5 (4)   A. Initial consonants

____/5 (4)   B. Final consonants

____/5 (4)   C. Short-vowel word

____/5 (4)   D. Long-vowel word

Instructional Needs

Skills to review: _____

_____

_____

_____

_____

Skills to teach: _____

_____

_____

_____

_____

Note: *Numbers within parentheses show benchmarks for on-level performance.*

TASK 1.   **Beginning Sounds**

Say to the student: *Words can begin with the same sound. Listen to these words:* boy, ball, *and* balloon. *All of these words begin with the same sound,* /b/* — boy, ball, balloon, /b/.

Practice Items

ride — *Tell me a word that begins with the same sound as* ride, /r/.
(If necessary, give examples: *The words* red, race, rhyme, run, Roger *all begin with* /r/.)

jam — *Tell me a word that begins with the same sound as* jam, /j/.
(Examples: *The words* jet, jump, just, job, Jill *all begin with* /j/.)

girl — *Tell me a word that begins with the same sound as* girl, /g/.
(Examples: *The words* give, get, go, game, Garfield *all begin with* /g/.)

Assessment Items Do not provide any help with the items below.

Recording On the lines below, indicate correct responses with a ✓. If a child gives an incorrect word, write that word. If a child gives a sound, write the letter that represents the sound between two slash marks, for example, /r/. Write **0** if a child does not respond. Discontinue testing if a child misses three consecutive items after the Practice Items.

_____, *Tell me a word that begins with the same sound as* _____, /_ /.

1. *sink, /s/* _____

2. *pie, /p/* _____

3. *more, /m/* _____

4. *donkey, /d/* _____

5. *lion, /l/* _____

6. *fast, /f/* _____

7. *children, /ch/* _____

8. *balloon, /b/* _____

____/8

*****Note:** *Whenever a letter appears between two slash marks, as /b/, the person giving this test should say the sound for this letter, not the name of the letter.*

TASK 2.   **Phoneme Blending**

Say to the student: *Words are made by putting sounds together. I am going to say the sounds, and I want you to tell me what word they make. For example, /s/ /a/ /t/ make the word* sat.

Practice Items

/b/ /e/ /d/ *What word would I have if I put together the sounds /b/ /e/ /d/?*
(If needed, **say:** /b/ /e/ /d/ makes bed.)

/m/ /a/ /p/ *What word would I have if I put together the sounds /m/ /a/ /p/?*
(If needed, **say:** /m/ /a/ /p/ makes map.)

/l/ /o/ /s/ /t/ *What word would I have if I put together the sounds /l/ /o/ /s/ /t/?*
(If needed, **say:** /l/ /o/ /s/ /t/ makes lost.)

Assessment Items Provide no additional help with the items below.

Recording Indicate correct responses with a ✓. If a child gives an incorrect word, write that word. If a child gives a sound, write the letter that represents the sound between two slash marks, for example, /r/. Write **0** if a child does not respond. Discontinue testing if a child misses three consecutive items after the Practice Items.

/_/ /_/ /_/ What word would I have if I put together the sounds /_/ /_/ /_/ ?

1. **/t/ /a/ /p/** *(tap)* _____

2. **/m/ /e/ /n/** *(men)* _____

3. **/j/ /o/ /g/** *(jog)* _____

4. **/k/ /u/ /t/** *(cut)* _____

5. **/l/ /i/ /d/** *(lid)* _____

6. **/b/ /i/ /k/** *(bike)* _____

7. **/w/ /a/ /v/** *(wave)* _____

8. **/s/ /o/ /f/ /t/** *(soft)* _____

_____/8

TASK 3. **Phoneme Segmentation**

Say to the student: *Now I will say a word and I want you to tell me the sounds that are in the word. For example, if I said* sat, *you would say /s/ /ă/ /t/.*

Practice Items *What are the sounds in* mud? *Think about the first sound, the next sound, and the last sound.* (If necessary **say:** *the sounds in* mud *are /m/ /ŭ/ /d/.*)

What are the sounds in not? *Think about the first sound, the next sound, and the last sound.* (If necessary **say:** *the sounds in* not *are /n/ /ŏ/ /t/.*)

What are the sounds in jump? *Think about the first sound, the next sound, and the last sound.* (If necessary **say:** *the sounds in* jump *are /j/ /ŭ/ /m/ /p/.*)

Assessment Items Provide no additional help with the items below.

Recording On the lines below, indicate correct responses with ✓. If a child gives an incorrect word, write that word. If a child gives a sound, write the letter that sound represents between two slash marks, for example, /r/. Write **0** if a child does not respond. Discontinue testing if a child misses three consecutive items after the Practice Items.

What are the sounds in _____ ?

1. *pat* (/p/ /ă/ /t/) _____

2. *leg* (/l/ /ĕ/ /g/) _____

3. *sip* (/s/ /ĭ/ /p/) _____

4. *tub* (/t/ /ŭ/ /b/) _____

5. *rock* (/r/ /ŏ/ /k/) _____

6. *mean* (/m/ /ē/ /n/) _____

7. *joke* (/j/ /ō/ /k/) _____

8. *fast* (/f/ /ă/ /s/ /t/) _____

TASK 4.   **Letter names—Uppercase**

MATERIALS: Student Page 1 (Blackline Master 11)

Say to the student: *Tell me the names of these letters.* Circle all incorrect responses. If the student cannot name three or more consecutive letters, **say:** *Look at all of the letters and tell me which ones you do know.*

	D	A	N	S	X	Z	J	L	H
	T	Y	E	C	O	M	R	P	W
___/26	K	U	G	B	F	Q	V	I	

TASK 5.   **Letter names—Lowercase**

MATERIALS: Student Page 1 (Blackline Master 11)

Say to the student: *Tell me the names of these letters.* Circle all incorrect responses. If the student cannot name three or more consecutive letters, **say:** *Look at all of the letters and tell me which ones you do know.*

	d	a	n	s	x	z	j	l	h
	t	y	e	c	o	m	r	p	w
___/26	k	u	g	b	f	q	v	i	

TASK 6.   **Consonant Sounds**

MATERIALS: Student Page 1 (Blackline Master 11)

Say to the student: *Look at these letters. Tell me the sound each letter stands for.* Ask if he or she knows of another sound for the letters *g* and *c*. If the sound given is correct, do not mark this form. If it is incorrect, write the sound the student gives above each letter. If no sound is given, circle the letter. If the student cannot say the sound for three or more consecutive letters, **say:** *Look at all of the letters and tell me which sounds you do know.*

	d	l	n	s	x	z	j
	t	y	p	c	h	m	r
___/23	k	w	g	b	f	q	v

TASK 7.　　　**Vowel Sounds**

MATERIALS: Student Page 1 (Blackline Master 11)

Say to the student: *Tell me the sounds of each letter.* If the student names the letter, count it as the long-vowel sound. Then **ask:** *Can you tell me the other sound for the letter?* The student should name the short-vowel sound.

e____ ____　　i____ ____　　a____ ____　　o____ ____　　u____ ____

l = long sound　　　　s = short sound

Record "l" on the first line for the long sound (letter name) and "s" for the short sound on the second line. If the student makes an error, record the error over the letter.

____/5　Long-vowel sounds (count the number of *l*'s above)

____/5　Short-vowel sounds (count the number of *s*'s above)

TASK 8.　　　**Reading and Decoding**

MATERIALS: Student Page 2 (Blackline Master 12)

For items A through G, students must read both real and pseudowords (made-up words). For the first line of real words, **tell the student:** *I want you to read these words.* If the student cannot read two or more of the real words, do not administer the line of pseudowords. Go to the next set of items. Before asking the student to read the line of pseudowords, **say:** *Now I want you to read some made-up words. Do not try to make them sound like real words.*

A.　Short vowels in CVC words

____/5	sip	cat	let	but	hog	(real)
____/5	vop	fut	dit	keb	laz	(pseudo)

B.　Short vowels, digraphs, and *-tch* trigraph

____/5	when	chop	rish	shut	match	(real)
____/5	wheck	shom	thax	pitch	chud	(pseudo)

C.　Consonant blends with short vowels

____/5	stop	trap	quit	spell	plan	(real)
____/5	stig	brab	qued	snop	dran	(pseudo)
____/5	clip	fast	sank	limp	held	(real)
____/5	frep	nast	wunk	kimp	jelt	(pseudo)

TASK 8.   **Reading and Decoding**
MATERIALS: Student Page 3 (Blackline Master 13)

D.   Long vowel spellings

| ____/5 | tape | key | lute | paid | feet | (real) |
| ____/5 | toe | bine | joad | vay | soat | (pseudo) |

E.   *r-* and *i-*controlled vowels

| ____/5 | bark | horn | chirp | term | cold | (real) |
| ____/5 | ferm | dall | gorf | murd | char | (pseudo) |

F.   Variant spellings and diphthongs

| ____/5 | few | down | toy | hawk | coin | (real) |
| ____/5 | voot | rew | fout | zoy | bawk | (pseudo) |

(**Note:** Student can pronounce *oo* in *voot* as in *moon* or *book*.)

TASK 8.   **Reading and Decoding**
MATERIALS: Student Page 4 (Blackline Master 14)

G.   Two-syllable words

Administer these items if the student is able to read most of the single-syllable real and pseudowords in the previous items. **Say to the student:** *Now I want you to read down the first column of words. Each of the real words in this column has two syllables.* Point to the first column. If the student can read at least three out of eight of the words in this column, **say:** *Now I want you to read some made-up words.* Point to the second column. Repeat the same procedure for the third column. **Note:** The following made-up words can be pronounced in two ways: *sunop* (*su-nop* or *sun-op*); *wopam* (*wo-pam* or *wop-am*); *potife* (*po-tife* or *pot-ife*); *zuride* (*zu-ride* or *zur-ide*); and *zubo* (*zu-bo* or *zub-o*). If words are read correctly, do not make any marks.

____/3	Closed	kidnap	pugnad	quilbrap
____/3	Silent *e*	compete	slifnate	prubkine
____/3	Open, closed	depend	sunop	wopam
____/3	Closed or open, open	zero	zubo	yodu
____/3	Open, silent *e*	locate	potife	zuride
____/3	Consonant-*le*	stable	grickle	morkle
____/3	*r-*controlled	further	tirper	pharbid
____/3	Vowel team	outlaw	doipnoe	loymaud

TASK 8. **Reading and Decoding**

MATERIALS: Student Page 4 (Blackline Master 14)

H. Multisyllabic Words

Administer these items only if the student is able to read six of the eight items in Task 8G, column 1. **Say to the student:** *Now I want you to read down the first column of words. Each of the real words in this column has more than two syllables.* Point to the first column. If the student can read at least three of the four words in this column, **say:** *Now I want you to read some made-up words.* Point to the second column. If the words are read correctly, make no marks. If words are read incorrectly, record the student's response above the word. Expected pronunciations for the pseudowords are given below the word.

_____/2 (Closed, unaccented, closed)   caravan   petimal
(pet i mel) or
(pe tim el)

_____/2 (*r*-controlled, unaccented, silent *e*)   marmalade   dorlishane
(dor li shane)

_____/2 (Open, closed, closed)   momentum   bolansun
(bo lan sun) or
(bol an sun)

_____/2 (Closed, unaccented, vowel team)   velveteen   matlopeen
(mat lo peen) or
(mat lop een)

TASK 9. Spelling

A. Give the student a pencil and a sheet of lined paper. **Tell the student:** *Number your paper from 1 through 5. Listen to each of the words I read and write the first sound you hear.* Write the student's responses over the words.

_____/5 1. fit 2. map 3. pen 4. kid 5. hand

B. **Tell the student:** *Number 1 through 5. Listen to each of the words I read, and write the first sound you hear.*

_____/5 1. rub 2. fled 3. leg 4. sell 5. less

C. **Tell the student:** *Number 1 through 10. Listen to each of the words I read, and write the whole word.*

1. fork   6. coin
2. yarn   7. float
3. sip   8. steep
4. shop   9. drive
5. tub   10. spoon

_____/5   _____/5

Phonemic Awareness and Phonics/Decoding Test

4.

D	A	N	S	X	Z	J	L	H
T	Y	E	C	O	M	R	P	W
K	U	G	B	F	Q	V	I	

5.

d	a	n	s	x	z	j	l	h
t	y	e	c	o	m	r	p	w
k	u	g	b	f	q	v	i	

6.

d	l	n	s	x	z	j
t	y	p	c	h	m	r
k	w	g	b	f	q	v

7.

e	i	a	o	u	

8. Reading and Decoding

A.

sip	cat	let	but	hog
vop	fut	dit	keb	laz

B.

when	chop	rich	shut	match
wheck	shom	thax	phitch	chud

C.

stop	trap	quit	spell	plan
stig	brab	qued	snop	dran
clip	fast	sank	limp	held
frep	nast	wunk	kimp	jelt

D.

tape	key	lute	paid	feet
loe	bine	joad	vay	soat

E.

bark	horn	chirp	term	cold
ferm	dall	gorf	murd	char

F.

few	down	toy	hawk	coin
voot	rew	fout	zoy	bawk

G.

kidnap	pugnad	quilbrap
compete	slifnate	prubkine
depend	sunop	wopam
zero	zubo	yodu
locate	potife	zuride
stable	grickle	morkle
further	tirper	pharbid
outlaw	doipnoe	loymaud

H.

caravan	petimel
marmalade	dorlishane
momentum	bolansun
velveteen	matlopeen

SECTION TWO:

Text Reading: Comprehension, Decoding, and Fluency

Administering and Scoring

SECTION TWO

What is the *Text Reading: Comprehension, Decoding, and Fluency* section?

Section Two of *Diagnostic Assessment* offers reading passages to help you observe reading skills and strategies applied to connected text and determine whether a student reads on, below, or above grade level. This portion of the test evaluates reading accuracy, reading rate and fluency, comprehension skills, and reading strategies.

Why administer this section of the test?

Using reading passages to assess a student's comprehension, decoding skills, and fluency provides insight into the student's strategies for understanding a passage and decoding words in context. This information reveals areas in which the student would benefit from explicit instruction.

- The scores for comprehension are based on the student's retelling and answers to questions, reveal how well the student understood the passage, and help you identify comprehension skills and strategies for further instruction and practice.

- There are two types of information useful for understanding a student's decoding abilities:

  1. a decoding accuracy score (percentage of words read correctly), and

  2. an analysis of the student's miscues (mistakes) and self-corrections.

     This specific information on strengths and needs reveals the student's strategies for reading words and helps you target skills for instruction.

- There are also two types of information useful for understanding fluency:

  1. reading rate, defined as Words Correct Per Minute (or WCPM), which indicates how quickly and accurately the student identifies words, and

  2. a fluency rubric, used to measure a student's ability to read with expression and in meaningful phrases, both of which reflect reading with comprehension.

What materials do I need for Section Two?	• **Recording Forms** for the narrative and informational passages at the appropriate levels. (See pages 48–89.) Permission is granted for reproducing these pages.
	• **Student Copy Blackline Masters** for the narrative and informational passages at the appropriate levels. (See pages 90–135.) Duplicate one set and mount each page on card stock or a folder for durability, if desired. Permission is granted for reproducing these pages.
	• **Stopwatch**, digital display, or clock with second hand
	• **Tape recorder** (optional)
	• **Calculator**

How long will the test take for each student?	• Individually administered
	• Ten to fifteen minutes per passage. (Time will vary, based on the number of passages a student reads.)
	• Administer both the narrative and the expository passages appropriate to the student's reading level. Passages are provided for the beginning of each grade, 1 through 6.

TEST ADMINISTRATION PROCEDURES

How do I administer the test?

Before Text Reading

Determine the level at which to begin testing based on your best judgment about a student's reading level and any additional information about the student's reading abilities. Generally, for struggling readers, begin with the passages that are at least one grade-level below the grade placement. If a student's accuracy score on the below grade-level passages is above 90%, the grade-level passages should also be administered.

Continue administering both the narrative and informational passages until you have found the student's *instructional level*, or the point at which the student's oral decoding accuracy and comprehension scores are within the benchmark scores for that level. (See pages 36–37.) You may need to use the next lower or higher passage to find the instructional level.

If performance on narrative and informational passages at the same grade level are quite different, use the overall average to determine instructional level.

During Text Reading

Begin the testing session by introducing this section of the test to the student.

> For Grades 1-2 **say**: *I am going to ask you to read some stories aloud to me. Read them as best you can. I can't help you, so if you come to a word you don't know, just try your best. When you're through reading each story, I will ask you to tell me about the whole story and I'll ask you some questions.*

> For Grades 3-6 **say**: *I am going to ask you to read some passages. I'll have you read the first part aloud and then you will read the rest silently—to yourself. Read aloud until I say "STOP." Then just continue to read the rest silently. Read as best you can, as if you were reading aloud in class. I can't help you, so if you come to a word you don't know, just try your best. When you're through reading, I am going to ask you to tell me about the whole passage and I'll ask you some questions.*

Present the student with the first passage and introduce it by reading aloud the information that appears after **Say** at the top of the Recording Form. This introduction allows you to preview any difficult concepts or words without interfering with the comprehension assessment that follows.

For passages at grades 1–2, students will read the entire text orally. For passages at grades 3–6, students will read aloud for the first 3 minutes and then continue to read silently. You will time the student and mark the place at which 3 minutes ended on the Recording Form. Have the student continue reading to the end of the sentence after 3 minutes. Then say "STOP," and ask the student to finish reading the passage silently. This procedure will allow you to calculate both decoding accuracy and words correct per minute scores.

Some teachers prefer to time students using three separate 1-minute sections rather than a single 3-minute section. If you choose to do this, mark the text at the end of 1 minute, 2 minutes, and 3 minutes.

As the student reads aloud, mark all miscues (errors) using the marking system provided. (See pages 33–34). Be sure to mark an X on the last word read at 3 minutes, or if you prefer, mark an X on the last word read at 1 minute, 2 minutes, and 3 minutes. If you have taped the student's reading, the tape can help you with scoring.

After Text Reading

After the student finishes reading, move the passage away for the retelling and comprehension questions so the student cannot refer to it. Begin with the retelling, using the prompt given on the Recording Form. Examples:

- (for fiction) *Now start at the beginning, and* you *tell* me *that story. Tell it in your own words.*

- (for nonfiction) *Now* you *tell* me *everything you remember from the selection about the great Yellowstone fire. Tell me in your own words.*

After the student's retelling, you should always ask, just once, if there is anything else. **Say**: *Anything else?*

Do not prompt the student beyond that, as it will interfere with an accurate evaluation of the retelling. Take notes as the student retells the story so you can use them later for scoring. (See page 35 for the Comprehension: Retelling Rubric). If you have taped the student's retelling, the tape can help you in the scoring.

After the retelling, read aloud to the student the Comprehension Questions found on the Recording Form. Record the score for each question. (See page 35 for further scoring information).

Tips
• Before students begin, remind them that you can't help them, that after reading they will retell the story in their own words, and that you will ask some questions.
• Time the reading in an inconspicuous way so that students are not tempted to rush through the reading, which may increase the number of errors and distract them from comprehension. Remember to mark an X on last word read on the Recording Sheet at the 3-minute time (or at 1 minute, 2 minutes, and 3 minutes). For passages at Grades 3–6, remember to let the student finish reading the sentence after you mark the 3-minute word and then say, "STOP." Tell the student to finish reading the passage silently.
• If the student stops at a word and resists continuing, wait three seconds and then prompt by saying, "Go on." Do not supply the word.
• Be sure to remove the reading passage before asking students to retell and answer the comprehension questions.

TEST SCORING PROCEDURES

How do I score Section Two: Text Reading?

Each Recording Form provides space for you to take notes and record scores, and it lists the simple steps for each calculation.

Decoding Accuracy

The decoding accuracy score indicates the percentage of words the student reads correctly. To determine the student's decoding accuracy score, record errors and self-corrections as follows. (Use your own marking system, if you prefer.)

- Any misread word is marked with a / through the word. Over the crossed-out word, write what the student said.

- Words left out are marked with a / through the omitted word.

- Extra words inserted by the student are marked with a ^. Write the inserted word(s) above the line.

- Self-corrections are marked with **SC** over the error mark.

All errors, whether they change the meaning or not, are counted as errors. Repetitions and self-corrections are *not* counted as errors. If the student self-corrects an error, the original error is not counted. If the student repeats the same error, count the error only once; for example, if the student repeatedly misreads *stallion* as *stallon*, only count 1 error. Mispronunciations of proper names are not counted as errors (e.g. *Doña Clara* as *Donna Claire*).

Scoring The measure of Decoding Accuracy helps you analyze the student's ability to decode words in text separately from the analysis of reading rate. To calculate the percent of decoding accuracy, follow the steps below.

- Mark the last word read at the end of 3 minutes with an X. Determine the number of words read in three minutes, using the cumulative word count at the end of the last line read and counting backward to the last word read. Record the total next to *Words in 3 Minutes*.

- Count the number of errors and record the total on the recording form next to *Minus errors*. Subtract and enter the *Total correct*.

- Divide the total correct by the number of words read (from line 1 under *Decoding Accuracy*) and enter the result.

- Multiply the answer by 100 to get the percentage, and record it on the form next to *% Correct*. This is the decoding accuracy score. At the student's instructional level, the score will be within 90–97%.

Later, when you record all the errors on the Scoring and Analysis Summary, you can look for patterns among them and gain useful information about decoding needs.

Fluency

There are two ways to gauge fluency from a student's oral reading of the passages. The first one focuses on reading rate, measured by the number of Words Correct Per Minute (WCPM). The second one focuses on phrasing and expression, or the reader's ability to group words and use expression to convey the meaning of the text effectively. Phrasing and expression reflect the student's attention to meaning *and* ability to decode.

Scoring Calculate and record the scores as follows.

Words Correct Per Minute (WCPM)

- Enter the number of words read in three minutes (also recorded above) on the Recording Form.

- Re-enter the number of errors and the total correct.

- Divide the number of correct words by 3 (for the three minutes of reading) to determine the average number of words correct in one minute.

- If you prefer to use three 1-minute readings, tally the words correct at the end of each minute and record the median (middle) value in the range. For example, if scores from three consecutive readings were 90 WCPM, 96 WCPM, and 93 WCPM, you would record 93 WCPM.

Note: Occasionally a student may finish a passage before the end of three minutes. If the scores for Decoding Accuracy and Comprehension are also above the on-level benchmarks, assume that the student is reading beyond the grade level tested and re-assess with a higher passage.

Phrasing and Expression

- Refer to the Fluency: Phrasing and Expression Rubric below. In general, students who score a 3 or 4 are judged to have adequate phrasing and expression. Those scoring 1 or 2 are exhibiting some difficulty. Note that students do not have to read flawlessly to score a 4.

- Enter the score on the Recording Form. You will probably find it easier to get an accurate score if you enter it immediately after the student's oral reading or after listening to the tape recording.

Fluency: Phrasing and Expression Rubric
4 = Reads primarily in larger, meaningful phrases. Although the student may make some errors, these do not detract from the overall structure of the story. Most of the story is read with expressive interpretation, guided by meaning and punctuation.
3 = Reads primarily in three- or four-word phrases, although there are some word-by-word slowdowns. However, the majority of phrasing seems appropriate and preserves the author's meaning. Some expressive interpretation is evident.
2 = Reads primarily in two-word phrases with some three- and four-word groupings. Some word-by-word reading may be present. Word groupings may seem awkward and unrelated to meaning. Little expressive interpretation is evident.
1 = Reads primarily word-by-word. Two or three-word phrases may occur occasionally, but these do not preserve meaning. No expression is evident.

Comprehension

Comprehension is assessed using both a retelling of the passages as well as five questions that students answer orally.

Scoring Calculate and record the scores as follows.

Retelling

- Consult your notes from the retelling.

- Use the rubric below to evaluate it.

Comprehension: Retelling Rubric
4 = Includes the main idea or problem, all significant events or information, many supporting details; retelling is organized in proper sequence and is coherent.
3 = Includes the main idea or problem, most significant events, some details; may include some minor misinformation; retelling is generally organized and sequenced.
2 = Has some information from the passage but misses the main idea or problem; may have a few key events, information, or details but not integrated into the larger story; little organization or sequence.
1 = Little or no content is included in the retelling; may include some points from the passage, mostly details, but misses the main idea or problem and significant ideas; retelling is unfocused, sketchy; misinformation or little information.

Comprehension Questions

- Consult the chart below for scoring the student's responses.

- Sample 2-point answers are on the Recording Form for your reference.

Comprehension: Questions
2 points = complete answer
1 point = partially correct answer (either not detailed enough or answering only one part of the question)
0 points = incorrect or no answer

Using the Results

How Do I Analyze Section Two: Text Reading?

Use the following steps to analyze each student's performance and plan instruction.

1. Use the Scoring and Analysis Summary (pages 46–47) to summarize the student's performance on the tasks.

2. Study the **sample case study** on pages 40–45 to help you use this process.

3. Locate your student's scores for comprehension and fluency in the chart on pages 36–37. Use the suggestions provided in the "What to do With Results" chart on pages 38–39 to plan instruction. Record your plans on the Scoring and Analysis Summary (pages 46–47).

Benchmarks for On-Level Performance

Grade/Passage Level		On-Level Performance
Beginning Grade 1 On-Level Passage	**DECODING ACCURACY** % Words Read Correctly	90–97%
	FLUENCY	
	Expression and Phrasing	3 points
	COMPREHENSION	
	Retelling	2–3 points
	Questions	5–6 points
Beginning Grade 2 On-Level Passage	**DECODING ACCURACY** % Words Read Correctly	90–97%
	FLUENCY	
	Rate: Words Correct per Minute	41–61 WCPM
	Expression and Phrasing	3 points
	COMPREHENSION	
	Retelling	2–3 points
	Questions	6–7 points
Beginning Grade 3 On-Level Passage	**DECODING ACCURACY** % Words Read Correctly	90–97%
	FLUENCY	
	Rate: Words Correct per Minute	61–81 WCPM
	Expression and Phrasing	3 points
	COMPREHENSION	
	Retelling	2–3 points
	Questions	6–7 points

Benchmarks for On-Level Performance

Grade/Passage Level		On-Level Performance
Beginning Grade 4 On-Level Passage	**DECODING ACCURACY** % Words Read Correctly	90–97%
	FLUENCY	
	Rate: Words Correct per Minute	84–104
	Expression and Phrasing	3 points
	COMPREHENSION	
	Retelling	2–3 points
	Questions	6–7 points
Beginning Grade 5 On-Level Passage	**DECODING ACCURACY** % Words Read Correctly	90–97%
	FLUENCY	
	Rate: Words Correct per Minute	100–120
	Expression and Phrasing	3 points
	COMPREHENSION	
	Retelling	2–3 points
	Questions	6–7 points
Beginning Grade 6 On-Level Passage	**DECODING ACCURACY** % Words Read Correctly	90–97%
	FLUENCY	
	Rate: Words Correct per Minute	117–137
	Expression and Phrasing	3 points
	COMPREHENSION	
	Retelling	2–3 points
	Questions	6–7 points

What to Do with the Results

The following chart provides suggestions for interpreting some common patterns in student performance on the Reading Passages and some suggestions for tailoring instruction to meet students' needs.

If a student is tested on a passage below grade level and scores well on measures for accuracy, fluency, and comprehension, arrange for another test session at the next higher grade level. Similarly, if a student demonstrates difficulty with several aspects of a passage, you may need to administer a lower level passage to get an accurate assessment of the student's skills and strategies.

If the student scores...	This suggests...
• below benchmarks for decoding accuracy, comprehension, and fluency for grade-level passage	The student will have difficulty with grade-level text and likely needs extra support in decoding. Examine the Scoring and Analysis Summary: Text Reading Errors to determine specific areas of word identification need. The student may also benefit from instruction in self-monitoring. Because it is difficult to determine comprehension and fluency abilities when students have difficulty with decoding, examine performance in these areas using a lower level passage.
• within or above benchmarks for comprehension • below benchmarks for decoding accuracy and fluency	The student is struggling with decoding yet still reads for meaning. He/she may rely too much on context and frequently self-correct, slowing fluency. This student will need extra support to read grade-level material and would benefit from easier texts. Additional decoding instruction is needed; look at the Scoring and Analysis Summary: Text Reading Errors to determine specific needs.

If the student scores...	This suggests...
• within or above benchmarks for comprehension and decoding accuracy • below benchmarks for fluency	The student is not automatic with word identification. This student would benefit from more time reading texts at his/her independent level and repeated reading.
• below benchmarks for comprehension • within or above for decoding accuracy and fluency	The student can decode but is having difficulty with comprehension. Examine the *words per minute* to be sure the student is not reading so fast that comprehension is suffering. Also, examine the performance on specific comprehension questions and the retelling to determine the nature of comprehension difficulty.
• on or above benchmarks for oral reading accuracy, comprehension, and fluency	This student is a strong reader. He/she would benefit from reading challenging text (above grade level) and most likely can read grade-level material independently or collaboratively.

Sample Case Study: Mark Lester

Name **Sample Case Study:** *Mark Lester*　　Date *11/22*

Say: I want you to read aloud part of a book called *The Midnight Fox.* It is about Tom, a boy who spends the summer on his Aunt Millie and Uncle Fred's farm. Tom has been watching a beautiful black fox and her cub in the woods all summer. Now Uncle Fred wants to get rid of the fox because she has been eating Aunt Millie's chickens. In this part of the story, Tom goes with Uncle Fred and his dog Happ to look for the fox.

Time the oral reading. Place an X on last word read at 3 minutes. Have student finish that sentence and then read silently to end.

The Midnight Fox

by Betsy Byars

	Cumulative Words
Uncle Fred crossed the creek in one leap—the water	10
was that low now—and stepped up the bank. ~~Silently~~ I *Suddenly*	21
followed. "Fox tracks," he said, and with the muzzle of his	32
gun he pointed down to the tiny ~~imprints~~ in the sand. I had *impronts*	45
not even noticed them.	49
If I had hoped that Uncle Fred was not going to be able	62
to find the black fox, I now gave up this hope once and for	76
all. What it had taken me weeks and a lucky accident to	88
accomplish, he would do in a ~~few~~ hours. *four SC*	96
"The fox must be up there in the woods," I said ~~eagerly,~~ *angerly*	108
knowing she was not, or that if she was, she had gone there	121
only to make a false track.	127
"Maybe," Uncle Fred said.	131
"Let's go there then," I said and I ~~sounded~~ like a *shouldn't*	142
~~quarrelsome~~, impatient child. *quarrel*	145
"Don't be in too big a hurry. Let's look a bit." . . .	156
I said again, "Why don't we go up in the woods and	157
look. I think the ~~fox's~~ up there." *fox is*	175

Name _Mark Lester_____ Date _11/22_____

The Midnight Fox (continued)

<u>Cumulative Words</u>

"I'm not looking for the fox," he said. "We could chase   186

~~the SC~~

~~that~~ fox all day and never get her. I'm looking for the den."   199

He walked a few feet ~~farther~~ *fast SC* and then ~~paused~~ *pushed*. He knelt and   211

(Long i, but proper names don't count)

held up a white feather. "One of Millie's chickens," he said.   222

"Hasn't been enough breeze in a week to blow it six inches.   234

Come on."   236

We walked on along the creek bank in the direction I had   248

other hoping

feared. I was now overtaken by a feeling of ~~utter hopelessness.~~   259

My shoulders felt very heavy and I thought I was going to   271

be sick. Usually when something terrible happened, I would   280

get sick, but this time I k~~e~~pt plodding along right behind   291

"STOP. Begin silent reading."

Uncle Fred. I could not get it out of my mind that the fox's   305

life might depend on me. I stumbled over a root, went down   317

on my knees, and scrambled to my feet. Uncle Fred looked   328

back long enough to see that I was still behind him and then   341

continued slowly, cautiously watching the ground, the woods,   349

everything. Nothing could escape those sharp eyes.   356

Suddenly we heard, from the woods above, the short high   366

bark I knew so well. The black fox! Uncle Fred lifted his head   379

and at once Happ left the creek bank and dashed away into   391

the woods. . . .   393

We walked up the field and then back to the creek.   404

We crossed the creek and while we were standing there   414

Happ returned. He was hot, dusty, panting. He lay down in   425

the shallow water of the creek with his legs stretched out   436

behind him and lapped slowly at the water.   444

The Midnight Fox (continued)

<u>Cumulative Words</u>

"Happ didn't get the fox," I said. Every time I spoke,	455
I had the feeling I was breaking a rule of hunting, but I	468
could not help myself. As soon as I had said this, we heard	481
the bark of the fox again. This time it seemed closer than	493
before. Uncle Fred shifted his gun in his hand, but he did	505
not raise it. Happ, however, rose at once to the call, dripping	517
wet, still panting from his last run. Nose to the ground, he	529
headed for the trees.	533
The sound of his baying faded as he ran deeper into the	545
woods. I knew the fox had nothing to fear from the hound.	557
The fox with her light quick movements could run from this	568
lumbering dog all day. It was Uncle Fred, moving closer and	579
closer to the den with every step, who would be the end of	592
the black fox.	595

3:15 to finish reading silently

Diagnostic Assessment
SECTION TWO

The Midnight Fox (continued)

Retelling
Say: Now start at the beginning, and *you* tell *me* that story. Tell it in your own words.

Sample Score 4 Retelling
Tom and Uncle Fred are walking in the woods looking for a fox. Uncle Fred sees fox tracks. Tom is afraid that Uncle Fred will find the fox. He tries to get Uncle Fred to go in the wrong direction, away from the fox. Uncle Fred finds a feather from Millie's chicken, so he thinks he is close to the fox's den. Tom tries to distract Uncle Fred by falling down. They hear the bark of the fox and the dog, Happ, runs after it. He comes back without the fox but then he runs after it again. Tom knows that the fox can get away from Happ but he worries that Uncle Fred will find the den.

Notes on student's retelling: *Tom and his uncle were looking for a fox. They were in the woods with their dog. The dog chased the fox. They found feathers. The fox had eaten a chicken.*

Comprehension Questions

1. What does Tom hope will happen?
   (Uncle Fred won't find the fox)

2. Why is Uncle Fred looking for the fox den and not for the fox?
   (so they would find the fox and would not have to chase it all over)

3. How does Tom feel as he walks with Uncle Fred?
   (He feels hopeless because he thinks Uncle Fred will find the fox.)

4. What two clues help Uncle Fred get closer and closer to the den?
   (the chicken feather and fox tracks)

5. Why doesn't Tom think Happ will catch the fox? *(The fox is too fast.)*

Scores

Decoding Accuracy

Words in 3 mins.		292
Minus errors	−	14
Total correct	=	278
Divide by line 1		0.95
Multiply by 100 (% correct)	=	95%

Fluency

Words Correct Per Minute

Words in 3 mins.		292
Minus errors	−	14
Total correct		278
Divide by 3	÷	3
WCPM	=	93%

Expression ___2___
(Rubric, page 34)

Comprehension

Retelling ___2___
(Rubric, page 35)

Questions ___4___
(Rubric, page 36)

Name Mark Lester _____ Date 11/22 _____

Scoring and Analysis Summary:
Text Reading

Indicate Levels: **B** = Below Benchmarks **W** = Within Benchmarks **A** = Above Benchmarks
(See chart, pages 35–37.)

Grade/ Passage No.	Date	Decoding Accuracy	Fluency: Words Correct Per Minute	Fluency: Phrasing, Expression	Comprehension: Retelling	Comprehension: Questions
Gr. 4 Passage 1	11/22	W	W	B	B	B

Overall Comments/Observations

Interest/Motivation: Mark read the story slowly and seemed disinterested. _____

_____

Understanding of Passages: Mark seemed confused. He got some of the main idea but missed that Tom wanted to

distract Uncle Fred from killing the fox. Many miscues affected the text's meaning. May need to check vocabulary.

Reading/Decoding Strategies: Mark has strong decoding skills. Many missed words were 2-3 syllables. That

might reflect unknown vocabulary since he didn't use context to self-correct those.

Fluency Rate and Phrasing/Expression: Mark's reading was choppy, with little expression. May reflect lack of

understanding or a need for more work on expressive reading. Rate is within 4th grade benchmarks.

General Comments: Mark is at 4th grade for decoding and WCPM, but expression/phrasing and

comprehension are below benchmark. Plans: Focus on vocabulary, inferential comprehension, retell-

ing/summarizing, and self-monitoring for meaning. Have Mark read independently in 3rd or 4th grade

texts for which he has background and vocabulary.

Overall Reading Level (check one)

☐ On Level/Instructional   ☑ Below Level/Struggling Reader   ☐ Above Level/Advanced

Scoring and Analysis Summary:
Text Reading Errors

Grade/ Passage No.	Text Said	Student Said	Did student self-correct?	Did the error make sense?	Was the error grammatically correct?
4/Passage 1	—	he	N	Y	Y
	Silently	Suddenly	N	Y	Y
	imprints	impronts	N	N	N
	accomplish	—	N	N	N
	few	four	Y		
	eagerly	angerly	N	N	Y
	then	—	N	Y	Y
	sounded	shouldn't	N	N	N
	quarrelsome	quarrel	N	N	N
	fox's	fox	N	Y	Y
	—	is	N	Y	Y
	that	the	Y		
	farther	fast	Y		
	paused	pushed	N	N	Y
	now	not	N	N	N
	utter	other	N	N	N
	hopelessness	hoping	N	N	Y

Oral Reading Diagnostic Checklist (A = Adequate Performance   L = Limited Performance)

A Consonants   L Syllabication   L Use of Context

A Clusters   A Prefixes/Suffixes   A Use of Punctuation

A Digraphs   A Use of Decoding   A Use of Grammatical

A Short Vowels   Strategies   Structure/Syntax

A Long Vowels/Vowel Pairs   L Use of Self-Correcting   L Phrasing in Thought Units
          Strategies   A Appropriate Rate

Analysis: Mark is below 4th grade level for comprehension but he is strong in decoding and rate of reading. His miscues suggest that vocabulary may be an issue as well as self-monitoring for comprehension. In addition, he seems to have difficulty with both literal and inferential comprehension.

Name _____ Date _____

Scoring and Analysis Summary: Text Reading

Indicate Levels: **B** = Below Benchmarks **W** = Within Benchmarks **A** = Above Benchmarks
(See chart, pages 35–37.)

Grade/ Passage No.	Date	Decoding Accuracy	Fluency: Words Correct Per Minute	Fluency: Phrasing, Expression	Comprehension: Retelling	Comprehension: Questions

Overall Comments/Observations

Interest/Motivation: _____

_____

Understanding of Passages: _____

_____

Reading/Decoding Strategies: _____

_____

Fluency Rate and Phrasing/Expression: _____

_____

General Comments: _____

_____

_____

_____

Overall Reading Level (check one)

☐ On Level/Instructional   ☐ Below Level/Struggling Reader   ☐ Above Level/Advanced

Name _____   Date _____

Scoring and Analysis Summary: Text Reading Errors

Grade/ Passage No.	Text Said	Student Said	Did student self-correct?	Did the error make sense?	Was the error grammatically correct?

Oral Reading Diagnostic Checklist (A = Adequate Performance   L = Limited Performance)

____ Consonants

____ Clusters

____ Digraphs

____ Short Vowels

____ Long Vowels/Vowel Pairs

____ Syllabication

____ Prefixes/Suffixes

____ Use of Decoding Strategies

____ Use of Self-Correcting Strategies

____ Use of Context

____ Use of Punctuation

____ Use of Grammatical Structure/Syntax

____ Phrasing in Thought Units

____ Appropriate Rate

Analysis: _____

_____

_____

_____

Text Reading

47

Scoring and Analysis Summary
Blackline Master 16

Say: I'm going to ask you to read a story called "Sam and His Pets." It is about a boy who has two different pets. Read the story and look at the pictures to find out what the boy's pets like to do.

Sam and His Pets

Sam likes Pal.

Pal is big.

Pal is fun.

Sam likes to play with Pal.

Sam and Pal play tag.

Pal likes to run.

He likes to get wet.

Sal is the cat.

Pal likes to play with Sal.

Sal runs to Sam for help.

Sal and Pal like this box.

Sal and Pal play in it.

The box is not big.

Can Sam fit in the box?

Sam hid the box.

What will Pal and Sal do now?

What will the pets play with?

Scores

Decoding Accuracy

Total words	85
Minus errors	– ____
Total correct	= ____
Divide by line 1	____
Multiply by 100 (% correct)	= ____
Types of errors	____
_____	

Fluency

Expression   ____
(Rubric, page 34)

Comprehension

Retelling   ____
(Rubric, page 35)

Questions   ____
(Rubric, page 35)

Retelling

Say: Now, start at the beginning and *you* tell *me* that story. Tell it in your own words.

Questions: 1. What does Sam like to do with Pal? (*He likes to play tag.*) **2.** Who helps Sal? (*Sam helps Sal.*) **3.** Where do Pal and Sal like to sit? (*Pal and Sal sit in a box.*) **4.** What do you think Pal and Sal will play with next? (*They will probably play with the ball.*)

Say: I'm going to ask you to read a selection called "Pigs."
Read each page and look at the pictures to learn about pigs.

Pigs

This is a pig.

Look at all the pigs.

The pigs are in a pen.

This pig likes the sun.

It sits in the sun in the pen.

This pig likes to dig.

It digs and digs in the pen.

This pig likes to get wet.

It digs in the mud in the pen.

This pig likes mud!

A big pig is a hog.

Can you find the hog in the mud?

All the pigs like to play in the pen.

Retelling

Say: Now, start at the beginning and *you* tell *me* that story.
Tell it in your own words.

Questions: 1. Where did one pig like to sit? (*Answers will vary. One pig sat in the pen, in the sun.*) **2.** Why might a pig like the sun? (*The sun makes the pig warm.*) **3.** What do pigs do in the mud and dirt? (*Pigs dig in the mud and dirt.*) **4.** What is the big pig called? (*A big pig is a hog.*)

Scores

Decoding Accuracy

Total words	81
Minus errors	− ____
Total correct	= ____
Divide by line 1	____
Multiply by 100 (% correct)	= ____
Types of errors	____

Fluency

Expression ____
(Rubric, page 34)

Comprehension

Retelling ____
(Rubric, page 35)

Questions ____
(Rubric, page 35)

Name _____ Date _____

Say: I want you to read aloud a story called "Looking After Billy." It is about two friends, a boy named Cal and a girl named Lucy, who baby-sit for a little boy named Billy.

Time the oral reading. Place an X on last word read at 3 minutes; student finishes passage orally.

Looking After Billy

	Cumulative Words
Cal and Lucy were very good friends. They lived next	10
door to each other and did many things together.	19
One day Cal and Lucy were playing out in back of Cal's	31
house. His mother came to the back door and called to	42
them. "I have some work to do," she said. "Would you be	54
willing to come in and look after the baby?"	63
Cal and Lucy were happy to help as long as it was the	76
two of them together. Then it would be more like playing	87
than helping.	89
"I'll be in my office," said Cal's mother. "If Billy starts	100
to cry, give him something to eat."	107

Looking After Billy (continued)

At first the baby was sleeping, so Cal and Lucy played a   119

game together. But Billy didn't sleep for long. And when he   130

saw the children playing, he started to cry.   138

"Your mother said to give him something to eat," said   148

Lucy. So Cal gave Billy something to eat. But that didn't   159

work. Billy wouldn't eat. He just went on crying.   168

"How can we get him to stop crying?" asked Lucy.   178

"I'll give him something to play with," said Cal. So Cal   189

gave Billy something to play with. But that didn't work.   199

Looking After Billy (continued)

<u>Cumulative Words</u>

"How can we get him to stop crying?" asked Lucy again. 210

"We can make funny faces," said Cal. So Cal and Lucy 221
made funny faces. But that didn't work. Billy couldn't see 231
the funny faces. He was crying too much. 239

"I give up!" said Cal. "How can we get him to stop crying?" 252

"Could we read to him?" asked Lucy. 259

"I never thought of that," said Cal. "But we can try and 271
see if it works." First Lucy read to Billy. And it worked! He 284
stopped crying! Cal read next and it still worked. Billy didn't 295
cry anymore. 297

Now when Lucy and Cal look after Billy, they read to 308
him. And Cal's mother always says, "You children can look 318
after Billy anytime you like!" 323

Name _____   Date _____

Looking After Billy (continued)

<u>Retelling</u>

Say: Now start at the beginning, and *you* tell *me* that story. Tell it in your own words.

Sample Score 4 Retelling

Cal and Lucy were playing in Cal's backyard. Cal's mother asked them to watch Cal's brother, Billy, while she did some work. Cal and Lucy played a game while Billy was sleeping. When Billy woke up, he started to cry. They tried to stop him from crying by giving him some food, a toy, and making funny faces. He finally stopped crying when they read to him.

Notes on student's retelling: _____

_____

_____

_____

Comprehension Questions

1. **Why did Cal's mom ask Lucy and Cal to look after Billy?**
   (*She had work to do.*)

2. **What did Cal's mom tell them to do if Billy cried?**
   (*Cal's mom told them to give Billy some food if he cried.*)

3. **What three things did Cal and Lucy try first to get Billy to stop crying?** (*They gave him food, a toy, and made funny faces.*)

4. **What did Cal and Lucy do that finally got Billy to stop crying?**
   (*They read to him.*)

5. **How did Cal's mother feel about the way the children took care of Billy?** (*She will let them watch Billy any time.*)

Scores

Decoding Accuracy

Words in 3 mins.		_____
Minus errors	−	_____
Total correct	=	_____
Divide by line 1		_____
Multiply by 100 (% correct)	=	_____

Fluency

Words Correct Per Minute

Words in 3 mins.		_____
Minus errors	−	_____
Total correct		_____
Divide by 3	÷	3
WCPM	=	_____

Expression _____
(Rubric, page 34)

Comprehension

Retelling _____
(Rubric, page 35)

Questions _____
(Rubric, page 35)

Say: I want you to read aloud a story called "The Elephant's Trunk." Have you ever seen an elephant or a picture of one? (Clarify that the elephant's trunk is its long nose.) This selection is about how the elephant can use its trunk for many different things.

Time the oral reading. Place an X on last word read at 3 minutes; student finishes passage orally.

The Elephant's Trunk

	Cumulative Words
The elephant has the longest nose of any animal in	10
the world. Its nose is called a trunk. The trunk helps the	22
elephant do many things.	26
The elephant can use its trunk for smelling. It can lift its	38
trunk way up in the air to smell if there is danger. It can tell	53
if animals or people are close by. Then it can run away or	66
hide so it won't get hurt. Sometimes elephants make a loud	77
noise with their trunks to tell other animals to run away, too.	89

The Elephant's Trunk (continued)

The trunk also helps the elephant to eat and drink. The   **100**
elephant can reach high up into the trees for food. The trunk   **112**
puts leaves into the elephant's mouth just like a spoon.   **122**

An elephant can also suck up water with its trunk.   **132**
But the elephant does not drink the water through its trunk.   **143**
It sprays the water into its mouth like a hose. Sometimes the   **155**
elephant sprays water and mud on its body. Water and mud   **166**
help keep the elephant cool when it is hot.   **175**

The Elephant's Trunk (continued)

Elephants also use their trunks for swimming under   **183**

water. An elephant just sticks its long trunk out of the water   **195**

like a snorkel to get air.   **201**

The trunk works like a hand, too. It even looks like it   **213**

has fingers on the end. It can pick up big, heavy logs or it   **227**

can pick up small things like a pencil.   **235**

What could *you* do with a nose like the elephant's trunk?   **246**

The Elephant's Trunk (continued)

<u>Retelling</u>
Say: Now start at the beginning, and *you* tell *me* that story. Tell it in your own words.

Sample Score 4 Retelling
The elephant's nose is called a trunk. It is the longest nose of any animal. The elephant uses its trunk to smell danger. Its trunk can also make a loud noise to scare animals and people away. The elephant uses its trunk to eat and drink. It will take leaves from trees and suck up water to put in its mouth. It sprays water and mud on its body with its trunk to keep cool. The elephant also uses its trunk for swimming. It sticks the trunk out of the water to get air. Elephants can lift heavy things with their trunks.

Notes on student's retelling: _____

_____

_____

_____

Comprehension Questions

1. How does an elephant use its trunk to tell if it is in danger?
   (*It can smell if animals or people are close by.*)

2. How do elephants use their trunks to get a drink of water?
   (*Elephants suck up water with their trunks and spray the water into their mouths.*)

3. Why do elephants spray themselves with mud and water?
   (*to cool off*)

4. How does an elephant use its trunk for swimming?
   (*It sticks its trunk above the water for air while it is swimming.*)

5. What does the selection say that helps you to know that elephants are strong? (*The elephant picks up heavy logs.*)

Scores

Decoding Accuracy
Words in 3 mins.		_____
Minus errors	−	_____
Total correct	=	_____
Divide by line 1		_____
Multiply by 100 (% correct)	=	_____

Fluency
Words Correct Per Minute
Words in 3 mins.		_____
Minus errors	−	_____
Total correct		_____
Divide by 3	÷	3
WCPM	=	_____

Expression _____
(Rubric, page 34)

Comprehension
Retelling _____
(Rubric, page 35)
Questions _____
(Rubric, page 35)

Say: I want you to read aloud part of a book called *A Chair for My Mother.*
It is about a girl who lives with her mother and grandma.
Point out the ellipsis. Say: The original book is much longer. These three
dots show where the book has more lines. Just keep reading when you come
to them.

Time the oral reading. Place an X on last word read at 3 minutes.
Have student finish that sentence and then read silently to end.

A Chair for My Mother
by Vera B. Williams

	Cumulative Words
My mother works as a waitress in the Blue Tile Diner.	11
After school sometimes I go to meet her there. Then her	22
boss Josephine gives me a job too. I wash the salts and	34
peppers and fill the ketchups. One time I peeled all the	45
onions for the onion soup. When I finish, Josephine says,	55
"Good work, honey," and pays me. And every time, I put	66
half of my money into the jar.	73
It takes a long time to fill a jar this big. Every day when	87
my mother comes home from work, I take down the jar. My	99
mama empties all her change from tips out of her purse for	111
me to count. Then we push all of the coins into the jar. . . .	124
When we can't get a single other coin into the jar, we	136
are going to take out all the money and go and buy a chair.	150
Yes, a chair. A wonderful, beautiful, fat, soft armchair. We	160
will get one covered in velvet with roses all over it. We are	173
going to get the best chair in the whole world.	183

A Chair for My Mother (continued)

That is because our old chairs burned up. There was | 193

a big fire in our other house. All our chairs burned. So did | 206

our sofa and so did everything else. That wasn't such a long | 218

time ago. | 220

My mother and I were coming home from buying new | 230

shoes. I had new sandals. She had new pumps. We were | 241

walking to our house from the bus. We were looking at | 252

everyone's tulips. She was saying she liked red tulips and I | 263

was saying I liked yellow ones. Then we came to our block. | 275

Right outside our house stood two big fire engines. I | 285

could see lots of smoke. Tall orange flames came out of the | 297

roof. All the neighbors stood in a bunch across the street. | 308

Mama grabbed my hand and we ran. My uncle Sandy saw | 319

us and ran to us. Mama yelled, "Where's Mother?" I yelled, | 330

"Where's my grandma?" My aunt Ida waved and shouted, | 339

"She's here, she's here. She's O.K. Don't worry." | 347

Grandma was all right. Our cat was safe too, though it | 358

took a while to find her. But everything else in our whole | 370

house was spoiled. What was left of the house was turned | 381

to charcoal and ashes. | 385

A Chair for My Mother (continued)

We went to stay with my mother's sister Aunt Ida	395
and Uncle Sandy. Then we were able to move into the	406
apartment downstairs. We painted the walls yellow. The	414
floors were all shiny. But the rooms were very empty.	424
The first day we moved in, the neighbors brought pizza	434
and cake and ice cream. And they brought a lot of other	446
things too. The family across the street brought a table and	457
three kitchen chairs. The very old man next door gave us a	469
bed from when his children were little. My other grandpa	479
brought us his beautiful rug. My mother's other sister,	488
Sally, had made us red and white curtains. Mama's boss,	498
Josephine, brought pots and pans, silverware and dishes.	506
My cousin brought me her own stuffed bear.	514
Everyone clapped when my grandma made a speech.	522
"You are all the kindest people," she said, "and we thank you	534
very, very much. It's lucky we're young and can start all over."	546

A Chair for My Mother (continued)

Scores

Retelling
Say: Now start at the beginning, and *you* tell *me* that story. Tell it in your own words.

Sample Score 4 Retelling
A little girl lives with her mother and grandma. Her mother works at a diner and the little girl helps out sometimes. She gets paid for filling the salt and pepper shakers. The little girl puts half of her money in a jar. Her mother puts her change in the jar too. They are saving to buy a big chair with roses on it. All of their furniture burned in a fire in their old apartment. Everyone was safe and they found a new place to live. A lot of people helped them by giving them furniture and food.

Notes on student's retelling: _____

_____

_____

_____

Comprehension Questions

1. **How does the girl try to help her mother?**
   (She works at the diner and saves the money she gets.)

2. **Why does the family need a new chair?**
   (All of their furniture burned in a fire.)

3. **Why were the mother and the girl afraid when they saw the fire?**
   (They thought something had happened to the grandma.)

4. **What did the neighbors and relatives do when the family moved into their new home? Tell two things.**
   (Any two of these: The neighbor man brought them a bed, the family across the street gave them a table and chairs, the grandfather gave them a rug, their aunt made them curtains, some neighbors brought them food, her cousin gave her a teddy bear, and Josephine gave them pots/pans and silverware.)

5. **Why did Grandma make a speech?**
   (She wanted to thank everyone for being so kind and generous.)

Scores

Decoding Accuracy

Words in 3 mins.	_____
Minus errors	− _____
Total correct	= _____
Divide by line 1	_____
Multiply by 100 (% correct)	= _____

Fluency

Words Correct Per Minute

Words in 3 mins.	_____
Minus errors	− _____
Total correct	_____
Divide by 3	÷ 3
WCPM	= _____

Expression _____
(Rubric, page 34)

Comprehension

Retelling _____
(Rubric, page 35)

Questions _____
(Rubric, page 35)

Name _____ Date _____

Say: I want you to read aloud part of a book called *An Octopus Is Amazing*. (Clarify that an octopus is a sea animal that has eight arms.) This selection tells how an octopus lives and what it can do.

Point out the ellipsis. Say: The original book is much longer. These three dots show where the book has more lines. Just keep reading when you come to them.

Time the oral reading. Place an X on last word read at 3 minutes. Have student finish that sentence and then read silently to end.

An Octopus Is Amazing
by Patricia Lauber

	Cumulative Words
An octopus is an animal that lives in the sea. It has a	13
soft, bag-shaped body and eight rubbery arms. The common	23
octopus lives in a den near shore. It may make its den in a	37
cave or a wrecked ship, in a shell or a tin can, under a rock	52
or in a crack in a rock.	59
Every octopus lives alone. Its den is small, just big	69
enough to hold the octopus. An octopus can squeeze into	79
a small space because it has no backbone. In fact, it has no	92
bones at all.	95

An Octopus is Amazing (continued)

An octopus can change color in a flash. Usually the   105

octopus matches its surroundings and is hard to see. If it   116

climbs into an empty shell, it turns pink and gray. If it crawls   129

among rocks and seaweeds, it may turn brown and gray and   140

green. An octopus can have colored spots or stripes. It can   151

be half one color and half another.   158

Color changes help an octopus to hide or to escape from   169

enemies. They may also show how an octopus is feeling.   179

Scientists say an angry octopus turns dark red. A frightened   189

one turns pale. An octopus that is enjoying a meal shows   200

pleasure by changing color. . . .   204

Sometimes an octopus leaves its den and hunts for   213

food. It hunts by sight, using its sharp eyes. The octopus   224

may crawl along, using its suckers to hold on to rocks and   236

pulling itself forward. Or it may jet, by drawing in water and   248

shooting it out through a tube, which is called the siphon.   259

With each spurt, the octopus jets through the sea.   268

Once the octopus spies something to eat, it spreads its   278

webbed arms. It floats down and wraps itself around its prey.   289

It may store crabs or clams in its suckers and take them   301

home to eat. When an octopus has eaten, it tidies up its den.   314

It clears out the shells, using its siphon to blow them away.   326

An Octopus is Amazing (continued)

Sometimes other animals try to eat an octopus. The	335
octopus does not fight. Instead, it tries to hide or escape. If a	448
big fish attacks, the octopus changes colors and jets off. The	459
octopus no longer looks like the animal the fish was going to	471
attack. And so the fish is fooled. An octopus can also give off	484
an ink-black liquid through its siphon. The ink forms a blob	496
that has the shape and smell of an octopus. The enemy attacks	508
the blob. The octopus, which has turned black, escapes.	517

Name _____ Date _____

An Octopus is Amazing (continued)

<u>Retelling</u>
Say: Now *you* tell *me* everything you remember from the selection about the octopus. Tell me in your own words.

Sample Score 4 Retelling
An octopus lives in the sea. It has a soft body and eight arms. It lives in caves or under rocks. It can squeeze into small places because it doesn't have backbone. An octopus can change color to hide from enemies. It can turn red when it is mad. It can crawl along the bottom of the ocean with its suckers. It can give off black ink that looks and smells like an octopus so it can escape.

Notes on student's retelling: _____

_____

_____

_____

Comprehension Questions

1. **Where does an octopus make its home?**
   (*Any of these is correct: in a den in a rock, in a shell or can, under a rock, in a cave, or a wrecked ship.*)

2. **Why can an octopus squeeze into a small space?**
   (*because it does not have a backbone*)

3. **According to scientists, what shows that an octopus is angry?**
   (*It turns dark red.*)

4. **How does an octopus catch its food?**
   (*It finds food by seeing it. It wraps its arms around the prey. It can store food in its suckers.*)

5. **How does the octopus hide from its enemies? Tell me two ways.**
   (*It changes color, hides, escapes, or gives off a black ink blob that its enemy attacks.*)

Scores

Decoding Accuracy

Words in 3 mins.	_____
Minus errors −	_____
Total correct =	_____
Divide by line 1	_____
Multiply by 100 (% correct) =	_____

Fluency

Words Correct Per Minute

Words in 3 mins.		_____
Minus errors	−	_____
Total correct		_____
Divide by 3	÷	3
WCPM	=	_____

Expression _____
(Rubric, page 34)

Comprehension
Retelling _____
(Rubric, page 35)
Questions _____
(Rubric, page 35)

Name _____ Date _____

Say: I want you to read aloud part of a book called *The Midnight Fox.* It is about Tom, a boy who spends the summer on his Aunt Millie and Uncle Fred's farm. Tom has been watching a beautiful black fox and her cub in the woods all summer. Now Uncle Fred wants to get rid of the fox because she has been eating Aunt Millie's chickens. In this part of the story, Tom goes with Uncle Fred and his dog Happ to look for the fox.

Time the oral reading. Place an X on last word read at 3 minutes. Have student finish that sentence and then read silently to end.

The Midnight Fox
by Betsy Byars

	Cumulative Words
Uncle Fred crossed the creek in one leap—the water	10
was that low now—and stepped up the bank. Silently I	21
followed. "Fox tracks," he said, and with the muzzle of his	32
gun he pointed down to the tiny imprints in the sand. I had	45
not even noticed them.	49
If I had hoped that Uncle Fred was not going to be able	62
to find the black fox, I now gave up this hope once and for	76
all. What it had taken me weeks and a lucky accident to	88
accomplish, he would do in a few hours.	96
"The fox must be up there in the woods," I said eagerly,	108
knowing she was not, or that if she was, she had gone there	121
only to make a false track.	127
"Maybe," Uncle Fred said.	131
"Let's go there then," I said and I sounded like a	142
quarrelsome, impatient child.	145
"Don't be in too big a hurry. Let's look a bit." . . .	156
I said again, "Why don't we go up in the woods and	168
look. I think the fox's up there."	175

The Midnight Fox (continued)

"I'm not looking for the fox," he said. "We could chase	186
that fox all day and never get her. I'm looking for the den."	199
He walked a few feet farther and then paused. He knelt and	211
held up a white feather. "One of Millie's chickens," he said.	222
"Hasn't been enough breeze in a week to blow it six inches.	234
Come on."	236
We walked on along the creek bank in the direction I had	248
feared. I was now overtaken by a feeling of utter hopelessness.	259
My shoulders felt very heavy and I thought I was going to	271
be sick. Usually when something terrible happened, I would	280
get sick, but this time I kept plodding along right behind	291
Uncle Fred. I could not get it out of my mind that the fox's	305
life might depend on me. I stumbled over a root, went down	317
on my knees, and scrambled to my feet. Uncle Fred looked	328
back long enough to see that I was still behind him and then	341
continued slowly, cautiously watching the ground, the woods,	349
everything. Nothing could escape those sharp eyes.	356
Suddenly we heard, from the woods above, the short high	366
bark I knew so well. The black fox! Uncle Fred lifted his head	379
and at once Happ left the creek bank and dashed away into	391
the woods. . . .	393
We walked up the field and then back to the creek.	404
We crossed the creek and while we were standing there	414
Happ returned. He was hot, dusty, panting. He lay down in	425
the shallow water of the creek with his legs stretched out	436
behind him and lapped slowly at the water.	444

The Midnight Fox (continued)

"Happ didn't get the fox," I said. Every time I spoke,	455
I had the feeling I was breaking a rule of hunting, but I	468
could not help myself. As soon as I had said this, we heard	481
the bark of the fox again. This time it seemed closer than	493
before. Uncle Fred shifted his gun in his hand, but he did	505
not raise it. Happ, however, rose at once to the call, dripping	517
wet, still panting from his last run. Nose to the ground, he	529
headed for the trees.	533
The sound of his baying faded as he ran deeper into the	545
woods. I knew the fox had nothing to fear from the hound.	557
The fox with her light quick movements could run from this	568
lumbering dog all day. It was Uncle Fred, moving closer and	579
closer to the den with every step, who would be the end of	592
the black fox.	595

The Midnight Fox (continued)

<u>Retelling</u>
Say: Now start at the beginning, and *you* tell *me* that story. Tell it in your own words.

Sample Score 4 Retelling
Tom and Uncle Fred are walking in the woods looking for a fox. Uncle Fred sees fox tracks. Tom is afraid that Uncle Fred will find the fox. He tries to get Uncle Fred to go in the wrong direction, away from the fox. Uncle Fred finds a feather from Millie's chicken, so he thinks he is close to the fox's den. Tom tries to distract Uncle Fred by falling down. They hear the bark of the fox and the dog, Happ, runs after it. He comes back without the fox but then he runs after it again. Tom knows that the fox can get away from Happ but he worries that Uncle Fred will find the den.

Notes on student's retelling: _____

_____

_____

Comprehension Questions

1. What does Tom hope will happen?
   (*Uncle Fred won't find the fox*)

2. Why is Uncle Fred looking for the fox den and not for the fox?
   (*so they would find the fox and would not have to chase it all over*)

3. How does Tom feel as he walks with Uncle Fred?
   (*He feels hopeless because he thinks Uncle Fred will find the fox.*)

4. What two clues help Uncle Fred get closer and closer to the den?
   (*the chicken feather and fox tracks*)

5. Why doesn't Tom think Happ will catch the fox? (*The fox is too fast.*)

Scores

Decoding Accuracy

Words in 3 mins.	_____
Minus errors	− _____
Total correct	= _____
Divide by line 1	_____
Multiply by 100 (% correct)	= _____

Fluency
Words Correct Per Minute

Words in 3 mins.	_____
Minus errors	− _____
Total correct	_____
Divide by 3	÷ 3
WCPM	= _____

Expression _____
(Rubric, page 34)

Comprehension
Retelling _____
(Rubric, page 35)

Questions _____
(Rubric, page 35)

Say: I want you to read aloud part of a book called *Tornado Alert*. (Clarify that tornadoes are powerful storms that happen in the United States every year.) This selection tells what tornadoes look like, how they are formed, and what they can do.
Point out the ellipsis. Say: The original book is much longer. Ellipses, or three dots, show where this part is shorter. Just keep reading when you come to them.

Time the oral reading. Place an X on last word read at 3 minutes. Have student finish that sentence and then read silently to end.

Tornado Alert
by Franklyn M. Branley

	Cumulative Words
Tornadoes are powerful storms. On a tornado day the	9
air is hot and still. Clouds build up rapidly. They get thick	21
and dark. In the distance there is thunder and lightning,	31
rain and hail. Here and there parts of the clouds seem to	43
reach toward the ground. Should these parts grow larger	52
and become funnel shaped, watch out. The funnels could	61
become tornadoes.	63
The funnel of a tornado is usually dark gray or black. It	75
may also be yellowish or red. The colors come from red and	87
yellow dirt picked up by the tornado as it moves along the	99
ground.	100
Tornadoes can strike most anywhere, but usually they	108
happen where there is a lot of flat land. Most tornadoes	119
occur in Texas, Oklahoma, Kansas, Nebraska, Iowa, and	127
Missouri. Florida also has a lot of tornadoes. Tornadoes can	137
touch down over seas and lakes. When that happens, they	147
are called waterspouts.	150

Tornado Alert (continued)

Most tornadoes occur during April, May, and June.	158
That's when cold air meets warm air near the Earth's	168
surface. The cold air pushes under the warm air. The warm	179
air is lighter than the cold air and rises rapidly. As the warm	192
air moves upward, it spins around, or twists. That's why	202
tornadoes are sometimes called twisters. Some people call	210
them cyclones. The wind speed around the funnel of the	220
tornado may reach 300 miles an hour. No other wind on	231
Earth blows that fast. . . .	235
During tornado season in the United States, there may	244
be 40 or 50 tornadoes in one week. Sometimes there are	255
many more. Most are small. Usually a tornado blows itself	265
out in less than an hour. Some last only a few seconds.	277
Small tornadoes do not travel far, and they cause little	287
damage. Big tornadoes destroy everything in their paths.	295
They may travel two hundred miles and last several hours.	305
During a tornado, there is thunder and lightning, rain	314
and hail. And there is lots of noise. It can sound as loud as a	329
freight train or a jet engine. The word *tornado* comes from	340
a Latin word that means thunder. Some of the noise does	351
come from thunder, but most of it comes from the roaring	362
wind. There is lots of noise, and lots and lots of wind.	374

Tornado Alert (continued)

Tornadoes are very powerful, and some cause a lot of	384
damage. Tornadoes can pick up branches and boards, stones	393
and bricks, cars, and sometimes people. They can rip off	403
roofs and leave a trail of wrecked houses. A tornado's path	414
may be only 20 or 30 feet wide. Or it might be 1000 feet or	429
more—maybe even a mile.	434
In 1931, a tornado in Minnesota lifted a train off its	445
tracks. The train and its passengers were carried through	454
the air and dropped 80 feet from the tracks. There were 170	466
people on board. Though many people were hurt, only one	476
person died. But in 1974, a series of tornadoes in Missouri,	487
Illinois, Indiana, and ten other states killed 315 people in	497
twenty-four hours.	500

Name _____ Date _____

Tornado Alert (continued)

<u>Retelling</u>

Say: Now *you* tell *me* everything you remember from the selection about tornadoes. Tell me in your own words.

Sample Score 4 Retelling

Tornadoes are powerful storms. They are usually dark gray. They can happen anywhere, but they usually happen where the land is flat, like in Texas. They happen most often in the spring when the cold air meets the warm air. There can be 40 or 50 tornadoes in one week. They are loud because of the wind. Tornadoes can cause a lot of damage. They can rip off roofs, pick up people, and even pick up trains.

Notes on student's retelling: _____

_____

_____

Comprehension Questions

1. **What is the weather like on a tornado day?**
   (The air is hot and still and clouds build up quickly.)

2. **What gives some tornadoes a yellowish or red color?**
   (from the dirt picked up by the tornado)

3. **Why do most tornadoes happen in April, May, and June?**
   (That is the time that cold air meets warm air near the Earth's surface.)

4. **What makes a tornado sound very loud?**
   (Most of the tornado's sound comes from the roaring wind.)

5. **What does it say in the selection that makes you know tornadoes are very powerful? Tell me two things.**
   (They can pick up cars, trains, and people; they rip off roofs; they cause a lot of damage.)

Scores

Decoding Accuracy

Words in 3 mins.		_____
Minus errors	−	_____
Total correct	=	_____
Divide by line 1		_____
Multiply by 100 (% correct)	=	_____

Fluency

Words Correct Per Minute

Words in 3 mins.		_____
Minus errors	−	_____
Total correct		_____
Divide by 3	÷	3
WCPM	=	_____

Expression _____
(Rubric, page 34)

Comprehension

Retelling _____
(Rubric, page 35)

Questions _____
(Rubric, page 35)

Blackline Master 42

Say: I want you to read aloud part of a book called *All for the Better*. This story takes place in 1933 when Evelina Lopez is eleven years old and leaving her family in Puerto Rico for the first time. It is the Great Depression, a time when many people lost their jobs and had no food to eat. Evelina's mother hopes she will have a better life in the United States. In this part of the story, Evelina has just gotten on the boat that will take her to New York. (Note that mispronunciations of names do not count as errors.)

**Time the oral reading. Place an X on last word read at 3 minutes.
Have student finish that sentence and then read silently to end.**

All for the Better
by Nicholasa Mohr

	Cumulative Words
The shrill whistle blared again as the ship slowly pulled	10
away from the dock and out into San Juan Harbor. Evelina	21
watched as first her mother and sisters and then her beautiful	32
Island disappeared from view. Soon the soft green-blue of the	43
Caribbean Sea and the cloudless bright sunny sky were all she	54
was able to see.	58
She wondered if she would ever again see the abundant	68
flowers and tall palm trees glistening in the bright sunshine.	78
Would she ever again bathe in Puerto Rico's blue waters or	89
walk along its white sandy beaches? Would she ever again bask	100
in the warmth of her beautiful tropical Island of Puerto Rico?	111
It was scary to think the answers to these questions might be no.	124
But the scariest part was being without her family. Evelina	134
hardly remembered her Tía Vicenta, who had left Puerto Rico	144
several years earlier. And she had never even met her aunt's	155
new husband. She felt as if she was going to live with strangers.	168
Evelina tried hard not to be too fearful about the future. Mami,	180
she told herself, had done what was best for *la familia*. So she	193
would do what she must to be brave.	201

All for the Better (continued)

Doña Clara, an acquaintance of her mother's, was also | 210

sailing on *El Ponce*. She had agreed to share a cabin with | 222

Evelina and to take charge of her during their voyage. | 232

During the first day at sea, Doña Clara was very | 242

attentive. She saw to it that Evelina was safely settled in | 253

her bunk and had all she needed to be comfortable. But the | 265

following day the sea grew rough and Doña Clara became | 275

seasick. She remained sick the entire voyage and never once | 285

left their cramped little cabin. | 290

It was Evelina who ended up taking care of Doña | 300

Clara. "You're an angel," Doña Clara whispered from her | 309

sickbed. "I'm the one who is supposed to be taking care | 320

of you." Then she insisted that Evelina mingle with the | 330

other passengers. Since Doña Clara slept most of the time, | 340

Evelina took her advice. But she always checked in on Doña | 351

Clara to make sure she was all right. | 359

Everyone remarked on what a thoughtful and | 366

responsible girl Evelina was. Her outgoing personality and | 374

good looks endeared her to all she met. "Evelina, come | 384

have dinner with us," they would say. Or, "Evelina, join us | 395

for a game of checkers." She was always sought after, and | 406

by the time the journey was over, Evelina had made many | 417

friends on board ship. | 421

All for the Better (continued)

To her surprise, on the last day of the voyage Evelina | **432**

felt sad. Sad about leaving *El Ponce*. Sad about saying | **442**

goodbye to Doña Clara and all her new friends. Everyone | **452**

had been so kind! They had taken her mind away from | **463**

her own sorrow. They had made the separation from her | **473**

mother and sisters seem less terrible, less fearful. | **481**

But now the voyage was coming to an end. Evelina | **491**

came up on deck. With all her might she wished that | **502**

El Ponce was entering San Juan Harbor, not New York | **512**

Harbor. She wanted to be back in Puerto Rico. | **521**

Evelina watched as this strange new city loomed gray | **530**

and forbidding. She cringed at the sight of the tall buildings | **541**

crowding across the horizon. Her heart sank as she looked | **551**

around. The city skies were dreary. The water had a foul, | **562**

oily smell. | **564**

A tug guided *El Ponce* to the dock. Evelina watched the | **575**

workmen move around the dock shouting strange words at | **584**

one another. They looped heavy ropes from the ship around | **594**

the dock's iron posts. Quickly *El Ponce* was tied fast and the | **606**

five-day journey was over. Doña Clara, who had recovered | **616**

as soon as they had neared land again, took Evelina's hand | **627**

to lead her ashore. They went down the gangplank onto the | **638**

docks of South Brooklyn. | **642**

All for the Better (continued)

Scores

Retelling
Say: Now start at the beginning, and *you* tell *me* that story. Tell it in your own words.

Decoding Accuracy
Words in 3 mins. _____
Minus errors – _____
Total correct = _____
Divide by line 1 _____
Multiply by 100
(% correct) = _____

Sample Score 4 Retelling
Evelina's mother arranged for her to leave Puerto Rico and go to live with her aunt and uncle in New York City. She had to take a boat there. Evelina was sad to leave her family and all of the things that she loved in Puerto Rico. A friend of her mother's, Doña Clara, made the trip with her. Doña Clara got seasick, so Evelina had to take care of her. Evelina ate dinner and played checkers with other people on the boat. She made many new friends. When the boat got to New York, she was sad to leave her new friends.

Fluency
Words Correct Per Minute
Words in 3 mins. _____
Minus errors – _____
Total correct _____
Divide by 3 ÷ 3
WCPM = _____

Notes on student's retelling: _____
_____
_____
_____

Expression _____
(Rubric, page 34)

Comprehension Questions

1. Name two things Evelina will miss about Puerto Rico.
(*her family, the flowers and palm trees, sandy beaches, blue waters*)

Comprehension
Retelling _____
(Rubric, page 35)
Questions _____
(Rubric, page 35)

2. Why does Evelina feel like she is going to live with strangers?
(*She could not remember her aunt and she had never met her aunt's new husband.*)

3. How does Evelina spend her days on the ship?
(*She meets a lot of people, she plays checkers, eats, takes care of Doña Clara*)

4. Why is Evelina sad about leaving the ship?
(*She did not want to leave her new friends.*)

5. From what you read in the story, how is New York different from Puerto Rico? (*New York has tall buildings, dreary gray skies, and dirty water, while Puerto Rico has sandy beaches, bright skies, and lots of flowers and trees.*)

Say: I want you to read aloud part of a book called *Rattlesnakes*. Have you heard about rattlesnakes? They are a special kind of snake. This selection tells interesting facts about them.

Time the oral reading. Place an X on last word read at 3 minutes. Have student finish that sentence and then read silently to end.

Rattlesnakes
by Russell Freedman

Cumulative Words

In rattlesnake country a dark cave in the side of a cliff	12
might be a rattlesnake den. Rattlesnakes come to the cave	22
when summer ends. On warm days they stretch out on the	33
rocks and soak up the autumn sun.	40
As the days get colder, the snakes crawl deep inside	50
the cave, where the frost can't reach them. They coil their	61
bodies together into a great ball of snakes. Then they fall	72
asleep, or hibernate, all winter long. Rattlers often share	81
their dens with copperheads, milk snakes, garter snakes, and	90
other kinds of snakes. Hundreds of snakes may spend the	100
winter sleeping together in the same cave.	107
When spring comes, they wake up, and as the warm	117
weather sets in, they leave their winter den for good. They	128
crawl off in all directions, ready to prowl for food and mates.	140

Rattlesnakes (continued)

Rattlesnakes are found only in the Americas, especially 148

in the United States and Mexico. They live in all sorts 159

of wild country—in forests, prairies, and deserts; in thick 169

underbrush and on rocky mountain slopes. There are 177

fifteen kinds of rattlesnakes on the United States mainland. 186

The biggest is the eastern diamondback. It can be up to 197

eight feet long! The smallest is the scrappy little pigmy 207

rattlesnake, which is less than two feet long. 215

Rattlers are pit vipers, a family of poisonous snakes that 225

have thick bodies, narrow necks, and big, wedge-shaped 234

heads. Pit vipers get their name from the pits in their 245

cheeks, which they use to hunt warm-blooded animals like 255

birds and mice. The pits sense heat. They tell the snake 266

if an animal is nearby or how far away it is. Guided by its 280

pits, a rattlesnake can strike at warm-blooded prey in total 291

darkness. And it will hit its target every time. 300

One thing sets a rattlesnake apart from all other 309

snakes—its rattle. When a rattler is born, it has no rattle. 321

Instead, it has a small, hard button at the tip of its tail. The 335

first time the young rattlesnake sheds its skin, it loses its 346

baby-button and gains its first real rattle. From then on, a 358

new rattle appears every time the snake sheds its skin. Each 369

rattle is a dry, hollow scale connected loosely to the rattles 380

on either side. 383

Rattlesnakes (continued)

Hearing a snake rattle in the wilderness can be very	393
frightening. At first it sounds as if dried bones are being	404
clicked together very rapidly. Then, as the rattler shakes its	414
tail faster, it sounds more like the angry buzz of an insect	426
or the hiss of escaping steam. This sound is a warning. A	438
rattlesnake shakes its tail to scare off enemies and give itself	449
time to escape. Its rattle can save the snake from being	460
stepped on by a horse or attacked by a dog.	470
A rattlesnake's fangs are as sharp as a doctor's needle.	480
When the fangs aren't being used, they fold back against the	491
roof of the mouth. As the rattler opens its mouth to strike,	503
the fangs spring forward and snap into place. A hollow tube	514
carries poison from a gland in the rattler's cheek to a small	526
hole at the tip of each fang.	533

Text Reading: Grade 5, Passage 2

80

Recording Form for Passage 2
Blackline Master 49

Name _____ Date _____

Rattlesnakes (continued)

Retelling

Say: Now *you* tell *me* everything you remember from the selection about rattlesnakes. Tell me in your own words.

Sample Score 4 Retelling

Rattlesnakes spend the winter in caves. They share their dens with other snakes. They are found only in the Americas. They live in all kinds of wild country. There are fifteen kinds of rattlesnakes in the United States. They are poisonous. They have pits in their cheeks that sense heat, which help them hunt for food. They have a rattle on their tails that can frighten animals and people away. Their fangs are really sharp, and the fangs carry poison from the snake's cheeks.

Notes on student's retelling: _____

_____

_____

_____

Comprehension Questions

1. What are two things rattlesnakes do in the winter?
   (They crawl into their caves; they coil their bodies together; they sleep.)

2. How do the pits in the cheeks of a rattlesnake help it catch food?
   (The pits can sense heat of nearby animals so the snake can strike.)

3. How does the rattlesnake get its rattle?
   (After it sheds its skin the first time, a rattle appears.)

4. Why are its rattles important to a rattlesnake?
   (The rattle scares off enemies. It saves the snake from being stepped on by horses or attacked by dogs.)

5. How does poison get from the rattlesnake into its victim?
   (A hollow tube carries poison from the snake's cheek to a hole in the tip of the fang. When the snake bites, the poison is released through the fang.)

Scores

Decoding Accuracy

Words in 3 mins. _____

Minus errors − _____

Total correct = _____

Divide by line 1 _____

Multiply by 100
(% correct) = _____

Fluency

Words Correct Per Minute

Words in 3 mins. _____

Minus errors − _____

Total correct _____

Divide by 3 ÷ 3

WCPM = _____

Expression _____
(Rubric, page 34)

Comprehension

Retelling _____
(Rubric, page 35)

Questions _____
(Rubric, page 35)

Name _____ Date _____

Say: I want you to read aloud part of a Greek myth called *The Girl Who Cried Flowers*. Do you know what Greek myths are? (Clarify that they are stories the ancient Greeks made up to explain the natural world.) This is a tale about a girl named Olivia who has a special gift and how a man named Panos responds to it.

Time the oral reading. Place an X on last word read at 3 minutes. Have student finish that sentence and then read silently to end.

The Girl Who Cried Flowers
by Jane Yolen

	Cumulative Words
In ancient Greece, where the spirits of beautiful women were	10
said to dwell in trees, a girl was born who cried flowers. Tears never	24
fell from her eyes. Instead blossoms cascaded down her cheeks:	34
scarlet, gold, and blue in the spring, and snow-white in the fall.	47
No one knew her real mother and father. She had been found	59
one day wrapped in a blanket of woven grasses in the crook of an	73
olive tree. The shepherd who found her called her Olivia after the	85
tree and brought her home to his childless wife. Olivia lived with	97
them as their daughter, and grew into a beautiful girl.	107
At first her strangeness frightened the villagers. But after a	117
while, Olivia charmed them all with her gentle, giving nature. It	128
was not long before the villagers were showing her off to any	140
traveler who passed their way. For every stranger, Olivia would	150
squeeze a tiny tear-blossom from her eyes. And that is how her	163
fame spread throughout the land.	168
But soon a tiny tear-blossom was not enough. Young men	179
wanted nosegays to give to the girls they courted. Young women	190
wanted garlands to twine in their hair. The priests asked for	201
bouquets to bank their altars. And old men and women begged	212
funeral wreaths against the time of their deaths.	220

The Girl Who Cried Flowers (continued)

To all these requests, Olivia said yes, and so she had to spend	233
her days thinking sad thoughts, listening to tragic tales, and crying	244
mountains of flowers to make other people happy. Still, she did	255
not complain, for above all things Olivia loved making other people	266
happy—even though it made her sad.	273
Then one day, when she was out in her garden looking at the far	287
mountains and trying to think of sad things to fill her mind, a young	301
man came by. He was strong enough for two, but wise enough to ask	315
for help when he needed it. He had heard of Olivia's magical tears	328
and had come to beg a garland for his own proud sweetheart.	340
But when he saw Olivia, the thought of his proud sweetheart	351
went entirely out of the young man's mind. He sat down by Olivia's	364
feet and started to tell her tales, for though he was a farmer, he had	379
the gift of telling that only true storytellers have. Soon Olivia was	391
smiling, then laughing in delight, as the tales rolled off his tongue.	403
"Stop," she said at last. "I do not even know your name."	415
"I am called Panos," he said.	421
"Then, Panos, if you must tell me tales—and indeed I hope you	434
never stop—tell me sad ones. I must fill myself with sorrow if I am to	450
give you what you want."	455
"I want only you," he said, for his errand had been long forgotten.	468
"And that is a joyous thing."	474

The Girl Who Cried Flowers (continued)

For a time it was true. Panos and Olivia were married and	486
lived happily in a small house at the end of the village. Panos	499
worked long hours in the fields while Olivia kept their home	510
neat and spotless. In the evenings they laughed together over	520
Panos' stories or over the happenings of the day, for Panos had	532
forbidden Olivia ever to cry again. He said it made him sad to	545
see her sad. And as she wanted only to make him happy, Olivia	558
never let even the smallest tear come to her eyes.	568
But one day, an old lady waited until Panos had gone off to	581
the fields and then came to Olivia's house to borrow a cup of oil.	595
"How goes it?" asked Olivia innocently, for since her	604
marriage to Panos, she had all but forsaken the villagers. And	615
indeed, since she would not cry flowers for them, the villagers	626
had forsaken her in return.	631
The old lady sighed. She was fine, she explained, but for	642
one small thing. Her granddaughter was being married in the	652
morning and needed a crown of blue and gold flowers. But,	663
the crafty old lady said, since Olivia was forbidden to cry any	675
more blossoms, her granddaughter would have to go to the	685
wedding with none.	688
"If only I could make her just one small crown," thought	699
Olivia. She became so sad at the thought that she could not give	712
the girl flowers without hurting Panos that tears came unbidden	722
to her eyes. They welled up, and as they started down her	734
cheeks, they turned to petals and fluttered to the floor.	744
The old lady quickly gathered up the blossoms and,	753
without a word more, left for home.	760

The Girl Who Cried Flowers (continued)

Retelling

Say: Now start at the beginning, and *you* tell *me* that story. Tell it in your own words.

Sample Score 4 Retelling

In ancient Greece, there was a woman named Olivia. When she cried, her tears were flowers. People came from all around so she could make them bouquets and garlands of flowers. She always had to think sad thoughts so she could cry to make the flowers. One day she met Panos. He fell in love with her as soon as he saw her. He told her stories and forgot about the reason he had come to see her, which was to have her make a garland for his girlfriend. They were married and he asked her never to cry again because it made him sad. One day an old villager woman came to see Olivia. She told her that her granddaughter would not have a wedding crown because Olivia wouldn't cry anymore. Olivia was so sad because she knew if she cried it would hurt Panos. This made her so sad that she cried and the old woman picked up the blossoms that came from her eyes.

Notes on student's retelling: _____

_____

_____

Comprehension Questions

1. What was Olivia's special gift? (*She cried flowers.*)

2. How did Olivia feel about her special gift?
   (*She did not complain. She liked to make people happy.*)

3. Why did Panos first visit Olivia?
   (*He wanted a flower garland for his girlfriend.*)

4. Why did Panos forbid Olivia to cry?
   (*It made him sad to see her cry.*)

5. Why was it a problem for Olivia to help the old lady?
   (*If she made the flowers, she would hurt Panos.*)

Scores

Decoding Accuracy

Words in 3 mins. _____

Minus errors − _____

Total correct = _____

Divide by line 1 _____

Multiply by 100
(% correct) = _____

Fluency

Words Correct Per Minute

Words in 3 mins. _____

Minus errors − _____

Total correct _____

Divide by 3 ÷ 3

WCPM = _____

Expression _____
(Rubric, page 34)

Comprehension

Retelling _____
(Rubric, page 35)

Questions _____
(Rubric, page 35)

Say: I want you to read aloud part of a book called *The Great Yellowstone Fire*. Have you heard of Yellowstone National Park? (Clarify that it covers more than two million acres and is protected from hunters and loggers.) Park officials believe that forest fires are part of the natural cycle of the area, so they only fight fires started by humans or threatening to people or buildings. This selection is about what happened in 1988 when there was a huge fire in Yellowstone.

Time the oral reading. Place an X on last word read at 3 minutes.
Have student finish that sentence and then read silently to end.

The Great Yellowstone Fire
by Carole G. Vogel and Kathryn A. Goldner

	Cumulative Words
In 1988, park officials expected another normal fire season.	9
After a dry winter, spring precipitation was high. Fires ignited	19
by lightning all fizzled out. Then, in June, conditions changed.	29
The air turned hot and dry, and practically no rain fell. Day	41
after day, the sun beat down on Yellowstone. Lakes and streams	52
shrank. In the meadows, grasses shriveled. In the forests, dead	62
lodgepole pines and fallen branches became parched. Slowly,	70
the landscape changed from lush green to withered brown.	79
Thunderstorms rumbled across the park but brought no	87
rain. Lightning ignited many small fires. Some died quickly,	96
while others sprang to life. The fires burned unevenly,	105
scorching here, singeing there. They leapfrogged through the	113
forests, leaving patches of trees and ground cover untouched.	122
Pushed along by dry summer winds, the fires grew.	131
Just over the park boundary in Targhee National Forest,	140
woodcutters accidentally started another fire. The flames	147
quickly spread into Yellowstone. Firefighters battled this	154
blaze and several others that threatened buildings, but they	163
could not stop the fires.	168

Name _____ Date _____

The Great Yellowstone Fire (continued)

By midsummer, almost 9,000 acres of Yellowstone's 2.2 million | **177**
acres had burned. Fires raged through forests that had taken | **187**
hundreds of years to grow. No rain was expected for weeks, and | **199**
officials were worried. On July 15, they decided to fight all new | **211**
natural blazes. Within a week, they began to battle all existing ones, | **223**
as well. Yet the fires continued to spread. | **231**

Wildfires usually burn more slowly at night, then rev up with the | **243**
heat of day. But in the summer of 1988, dry night winds blew down | **257**
from high ridges, fanning the blazes. Day and night, ground fires | **268**
crackled through dead pine needles, branches, and logs, blackening | **277**
the forest floor. In some places, they scorched the bases of trees but | **290**
left the tops green. In other areas, the ground fires burned hotter and | **303**
toasted needles in the crowns of the trees a dusty rust color. . . . | **315**

From sunup to sunset and into the night, nearly 9,500 firefighters | **326**
from all parts of the country battled the blazes. Many of these men | **339**
and women prepared firebreaks. They cleared strips of ground of | **349**
everything that could burn. Sometimes they scraped the land | **358**
with hand tools; at other times, they detonated explosives or set | **369**
small backfires. They sprayed trees and buildings with water or | **379**
fire-retardant foam and snuffed out spot fires. | **387**

The Great Yellowstone Fire (continued)

To fight remote blazes, firefighters hiked into the — 395

backcountry. Smoke jumpers parachuted in. Sometimes — 401

fire crews dropped water or fire retardant onto the blazes — 411

from helicopters and airplanes. Yet the fires defied — 419

everyone's best efforts. Blazes subdued by water or — 427

retardant leapt back to life. Small fires grew and joined with — 438

bigger fires. Flames skipped over prepared firebreaks, roads, — 446

and rivers. One blaze even jumped the Grand Canyon of — 456

the Yellowstone River. By mid-August, experts agreed that — 465

only a change in weather could stop the fires. — 474

But the forecast for hot, dry weather remained — 482

unchanged. On August 20, the day that would be called — 492

Black Saturday, gale-force winds fanned every blaze in — 501

the park. Flames rampaged through forests and meadows. — 509

Smoke billowed high into the sky, and gray ash rained down. — 520

Powerless, firefighters could only stand and watch while — 528

fire consumed another 160,000 acres. More of Yellowstone — 536

was blackened on this one day than in the previous 116 years. — 548

The amount of burned area in the park had doubled. — 558

Name _____ Date _____

The Great Yellowstone Fire (continued)

Retelling
Say: Now *you* tell *me* everything you remember from the selection about the great Yellowstone fire. Tell me in your own words

Sample Score 4 Retelling
During the summer of 1988, it was dry and hot in Yellowstone. Lightning started small fires that grew into big ones. Some woodcutters also started a fire. The firefighters could not put out the fires. By July the fires were still burning. Firefighters from all over the country were fighting the fires by spraying water and foam. They hiked or parachuted into the forests to try to put out the fires. They dropped fire retardant from planes and made firebreaks. But nothing helped. They decided that the only thing that would work was a change in the weather. In August, the fires were still burning. The firefighters could not stop them. More of Yellowstone burned in one day than had burned in 116 years.

Notes on student's retelling: _____

_____

_____

_____

Comprehension Questions

1. From what you have read, name two things that caused fires to start in the summer of 1988. *(lightning and people)*

2. Why did the firefighters decide to fight all natural and new fires in July? *(because there was not going to be any rain)*

3. How did the firefighters try to put out the fires? *(They created firebreaks. They sprayed trees and buildings with water and foam and snuffed out spot fires. They parachuted into the fires or dropped water from helicopters.)*

4. What did the experts decide was the only hope to stop the fires? *(a change in the weather)*

5. Why is August 20, 1988 known as Black Saturday? *(Winds fanned all of the fires. More acres of Yellowstone burned that day than in 116 years.)*

Scores

Decoding Accuracy

Words in 3 mins.	_____
Minus errors	– _____
Total correct	= _____
Divide by line 1	_____
Multiply by 100 (% correct)	= _____

Fluency
Words Correct Per Minute

Words in 3 mins.		_____
Minus errors	–	_____
Total correct		_____
Divide by 3	÷	3
WCPM	=	_____

Expression _____
(Rubric, page 34)

Comprehension
Retelling _____
(Rubric, page 35)
Questions _____
(Rubric, page 35)

Name _____ Date _____

Sam and His Pets

Sam and His Pets (continued)

Sam likes Pal.

Pal is big.

Pal is fun.

Sam and His Pets (continued)

Sam likes to play with Pal.

Sam and Pal play tag.

Name _____ Date _____

Sam and His Pets (continued)

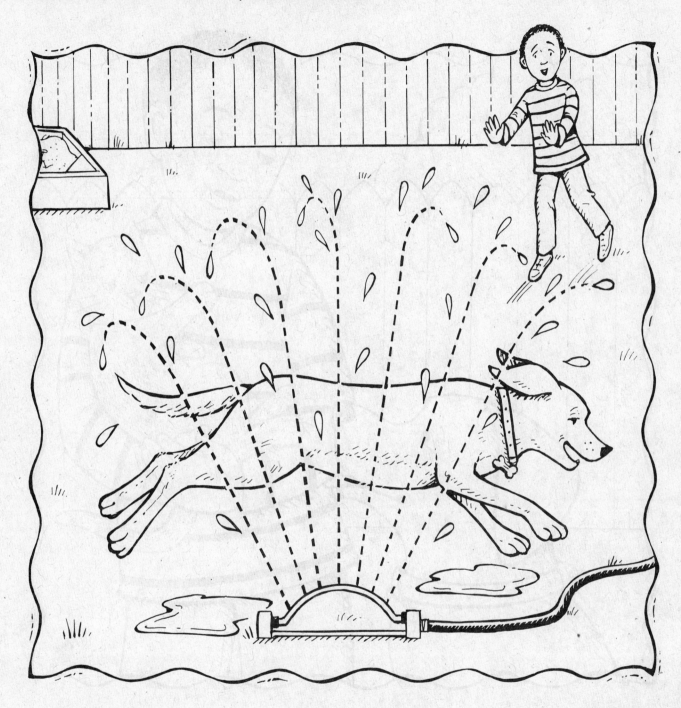

Pal likes to run.

He likes to get wet.

Sam and His Pets (continued)

Sal is the cat.

Pal likes to play with Sal.

Sal runs to Sam for help.

● **Sam and His Pets (continued)**

Sal and Pal like this box.

Sal and Pal play in it.

Sam and His Pets (continued)

The box is not big.

Can Sam fit in the box?

Sam and His Pets (continued)

Sam hid the box.

What will Pal and Sal do now?

What will the pets play with?

Pigs

Pigs (continued)

This is a pig.

Pigs (continued)

Look at all the pigs.

The pigs are in a pen.

Name _____ Date _____

Pigs (continued)

This pig likes the sun.

It sits in the sun in the pen.

Name _____   Date _____

Pigs (continued)

This pig likes to dig.

It digs and digs in the pen.

Name _____ Date _____

Pigs (continued)

This pig likes to get wet.

It digs in the mud in the pen.

This pig likes mud!

Pigs (continued)

A big pig is a hog.

Can you find the hog in the mud?

Pigs (continued)

All the pigs like to play in the pen.

Name _____ Date _____

Looking After Billy

Cal and Lucy were very good friends. They lived next door to each other and did many things together.

One day Cal and Lucy were playing out in back of Cal's house. His mother came to the back door and called to them. "I have some work to do," she said. "Would you be willing to come in and look after the baby?"

Cal and Lucy were happy to help as long as it was the two of them together. Then it would be more like playing than helping.

"I'll be in my office," said Cal's mother. "If Billy starts to cry, give him something to eat."

106

Looking After Billy (continued)

At first the baby was sleeping, so Cal and Lucy played a game together. But Billy didn't sleep for long. And when he saw the children playing, he started to cry.

"Your mother said to give him something to eat," said Lucy. So Cal gave Billy something to eat. But that didn't work. Billy wouldn't eat. He just went on crying.

"How can we get him to stop crying?" asked Lucy.

"I'll give him something to play with," said Cal. So Cal gave Billy something to play with. But that didn't work.

Looking After Billy (continued)

"How can we get him to stop crying?" asked Lucy again.

"We can make funny faces," said Cal. So Cal and Lucy made funny faces. But that didn't work. Billy couldn't see the funny faces. He was crying too much.

"I give up!" said Cal. "How can we get him to stop crying?"

"Could we read to him?" asked Lucy.

"I never thought of that," said Cal. "But we can try and see if it works." First Lucy read to Billy. And it worked! He stopped crying! Cal read next and it still worked. Billy didn't cry anymore.

Now when Lucy and Cal look after Billy, they read to him. And Cal's mother always says, "You children can look after Billy anytime you like!"

The Elephant's Trunk

The elephant has the longest nose of any animal in the world. Its nose is called a trunk. The trunk helps the elephant do many things.

The elephant can use its trunk for smelling. It can lift its trunk way up in the air to smell if there is danger. It can tell if animals or people are close by. Then it can run away or hide so it won't get hurt. Sometimes elephants make a loud noise with their trunks to tell other animals to run away, too.

The Elephant's Trunk (continued)

The trunk also helps the elephant to eat and drink. The elephant can reach high up into the trees for food. The trunk puts leaves into the elephant's mouth just like a spoon.

An elephant can also suck up water with its trunk. But the elephant does not drink the water through its trunk. It sprays the water into its mouth like a hose. Sometimes the elephant sprays water and mud on its body. Water and mud help keep the elephant cool when it is hot.

The Elephant's Trunk (continued)

Elephants also use their trunks for swimming under water. An elephant just sticks its long trunk out of the water like a snorkel to get air.

The trunk works like a hand, too. It even looks like it has fingers on the end. It can pick up big, heavy logs or it can pick up small things like a pencil.

What could *you* do with a nose like the elephant's trunk?

A Chair for My Mother

by Vera B. Williams

My mother works as a waitress in the Blue Tile Diner. After school sometimes I go to meet her there. Then her boss Josephine gives me a job too. I wash the salts and peppers and fill the ketchups. One time I peeled all the onions for the onion soup. When I finish, Josephine says, "Good work, honey," and pays me. And every time, I put half of my money into the jar.

It takes a long time to fill a jar this big. Every day when my mother comes home from work, I take down the jar. My mama empties all her change from tips out of her purse for me to count. Then we push all of the coins into the jar. ...

When we can't get a single other coin into the jar, we are going to take out all the money and go and buy a chair. Yes, a chair. A wonderful, beautiful, fat, soft armchair. We will get one covered in velvet with roses all over it. We are going to get the best chair in the whole world.

A Chair for My Mother (continued)

That is because our old chairs burned up. There was a big fire in our other house. All our chairs burned. So did our sofa and so did everything else. That wasn't such a long time ago.

My mother and I were coming home from buying new shoes. I had new sandals. She had new pumps. We were walking to our house from the bus. We were looking at everyone's tulips. She was saying she liked red tulips and I was saying I liked yellow ones. Then we came to our block.

Right outside our house stood two big fire engines. I could see lots of smoke. Tall orange flames came out of the roof. All the neighbors stood in a bunch across the street. Mama grabbed my hand and we ran. My uncle Sandy saw us and ran to us. Mama yelled, "Where's Mother?" I yelled, "Where's my grandma?" My aunt Ida waved and shouted, "She's here, she's here. She's O.K. Don't worry."

Grandma was all right. Our cat was safe too, though it took a while to find her. But everything else in our whole house was spoiled. What was left of the house was turned to charcoal and ashes.

A Chair for My Mother (continued)

We went to stay with my mother's sister Aunt Ida
and Uncle Sandy. Then we were able to move into the
apartment downstairs. We painted the walls yellow. The
floors were all shiny. But the rooms were very empty.

The first day we moved in, the neighbors brought pizza
and cake and ice cream. And they brought a lot of other
things too. The family across the street brought a table and
three kitchen chairs. The very old man next door gave us a
bed from when his children were little. My other grandpa
brought us his beautiful rug. My mother's other sister,
Sally, had made us red and white curtains. Mama's boss,
Josephine, brought pots and pans, silverware and dishes.
My cousin brought me her own stuffed bear.

Everyone clapped when my grandma made a speech.
"You are all the kindest people," she said, "and we thank you
very, very much. It's lucky we're young and can start all over."

An Octopus Is Amazing
by Patricia Lauber

An octopus is an animal that lives in the sea. It has a soft, bag-shaped body and eight rubbery arms. The common octopus lives in a den near shore. It may make its den in a cave or a wrecked ship, in a shell or a tin can, under a rock or in a crack in a rock.

Every octopus lives alone. Its den is small, just big enough to hold the octopus. An octopus can squeeze into a small space because it has no backbone. In fact, it has no bones at all.

An octopus can change color in a flash. Usually the octopus matches its surroundings and is hard to see. If it climbs into an empty shell, it turns pink and gray. If it crawls among rocks and seaweeds, it may turn brown and gray and green. An octopus can have colored spots or stripes. It can be half one color and half another.

An Octopus is Amazing (continued)

Color changes help an octopus to hide or to escape from enemies. They may also show how an octopus is feeling. Scientists say an angry octopus turns dark red. A frightened one turns pale. An octopus that is enjoying a meal shows pleasure by changing color. . . .

Sometimes an octopus leaves its den and hunts for food. It hunts by sight, using its sharp eyes. The octopus may crawl along, using its suckers to hold on to rocks and pulling itself forward. Or it may jet, by drawing in water and shooting it out through a tube, which is called the siphon. With each spurt, the octopus jets through the sea.

Once the octopus spies something to eat, it spreads its webbed arms. It floats down and wraps itself around its prey. It may store crabs or clams in its suckers and take them home to eat. When an octopus has eaten, it tidies up its den. It clears out the shells, using its siphon to blow them away.

An Octopus is Amazing (continued)

Sometimes other animals try to eat an octopus.
The octopus does not fight. Instead, it tries to hide or
escape. If a big fish attacks, the octopus changes colors and
jets off. The octopus no longer looks like the animal the fish
was going to attack. And so the fish is fooled. An octopus
can also give off an ink-black liquid through its siphon. The
ink forms a blob that has the shape and smell of an octopus.
The enemy attacks the blob. The octopus, which has turned
black, escapes.

The Midnight Fox

by Betsy Byars

Uncle Fred crossed the creek in one leap—the water was that low now—and stepped up the bank. Silently I followed. "Fox tracks," he said, and with the muzzle of his gun he pointed down to the tiny imprints in the sand. I had not even noticed them.

If I had hoped that Uncle Fred was not going to be able to find the black fox, I now gave up this hope once and for all. What it had taken me weeks and a lucky accident to accomplish, he would do in a few hours.

"The fox must be up there in the woods," I said eagerly, knowing she was not, or that if she was, she had gone there only to make a false track.

"Maybe," Uncle Fred said.

"Let's go there then," I said and I sounded like a quarrelsome, impatient child.

"Don't be in too big a hurry. Let's look a bit." . . .

I said again, "Why don't we go up in the woods and look. I think the fox's up there."

118

The Midnight Fox (continued)

"I'm not looking for the fox," he said. "We could chase that fox all day and never get her. I'm looking for the den." He walked a few feet farther and then paused. He knelt and held up a white feather. "One of Millie's chickens," he said. "Hasn't been enough breeze in a week to blow it six inches. Come on."

We walked on along the creek bank in the direction I had feared. I was now overtaken by a feeling of utter hopelessness. My shoulders felt very heavy and I thought I was going to be sick. Usually when something terrible happened, I would get sick, but this time I kept plodding along right behind Uncle Fred. I could not get it out of my mind that the fox's life might depend on me. I stumbled over a root, went down on my knees, and scrambled to my feet. Uncle Fred looked back long enough to see that I was still behind him and then continued slowly, cautiously watching the ground, the woods, everything. Nothing could escape those sharp eyes.

Suddenly we heard, from the woods above, the short high bark I knew so well. The black fox! Uncle Fred lifted his head and at once Happ left the creek bank and dashed away into the woods. . . .

We walked up the field and then back to the creek. We crossed the creek and while we were standing there Happ returned. He was hot, dusty, panting. He lay down in the shallow water of the creek with his legs stretched out behind him and lapped slowly at the water.

The Midnight Fox (continued)

"Happ didn't get the fox," I said. Every time I spoke, I had the feeling I was breaking a rule of hunting, but I could not help myself. As soon as I had said this, we heard the bark of the fox again. This time it seemed closer than before. Uncle Fred shifted his gun in his hand, but he did not raise it. Happ, however, rose at once to the call, dripping wet, still panting from his last run. Nose to the ground, he headed for the trees.

The sound of his baying faded as he ran deeper into the woods. I knew the fox had nothing to fear from the hound. The fox with her light quick movements could run from this lumbering dog all day. It was Uncle Fred, moving closer and closer to the den with every step, who would be the end of the black fox.

Tornado Alert
by Franklyn M. Branley

Tornadoes are powerful storms. On a tornado day the air is hot and still. Clouds build up rapidly. They get thick and dark. In the distance there is thunder and lightning, rain and hail. Here and there parts of the clouds seem to reach toward the ground. Should these parts grow larger and become funnel shaped, watch out. The funnels could become tornadoes.

The funnel of a tornado is usually dark gray or black. It may also be yellowish or red. The colors come from red and yellow dirt picked up by the tornado as it moves along the ground.

Tornadoes can strike most anywhere, but usually they happen where there is a lot of flat land. Most tornadoes occur in Texas, Oklahoma, Kansas, Nebraska, Iowa, and Missouri. Florida also has a lot of tornadoes. Tornadoes can touch down over seas and lakes. When that happens, they are called waterspouts.

Tornado Alert (continued)

Most tornadoes occur during April, May, and June. That's when cold air meets warm air near the Earth's surface. The cold air pushes under the warm air. The warm air is lighter than the cold air and rises rapidly. As the warm air moves upward, it spins around, or twists. That's why tornadoes are sometimes called twisters. Some people call them cyclones. The wind speed around the funnel of the tornado may reach 300 miles an hour. No other wind on Earth blows that fast. . . .

During tornado season in the United States, there may be 40 or 50 tornadoes in one week. Sometimes there are many more. Most are small. Usually a tornado blows itself out in less than an hour. Some last only a few seconds. Small tornadoes do not travel far, and they cause little damage. Big tornadoes destroy everything in their paths. They may travel two hundred miles and last several hours.

During a tornado, there is thunder and lightning, rain and hail. And there is lots of noise. It can sound as loud as a freight train or a jet engine. The word *tornado* comes from a Latin word that means thunder. Some of the noise does come from thunder, but most of it comes from the roaring wind. There is lots of noise, and lots and lots of wind.

Tornado Alert (continued)

Tornadoes are very powerful, and some cause a lot of damage. Tornadoes can pick up branches and boards, stones and bricks, cars, and sometimes people. They can rip off roofs and leave a trail of wrecked houses. A tornado's path may be only 20 or 30 feet wide. Or it might be 1000 feet or more—maybe even a mile.

In 1931, a tornado in Minnesota lifted a train off its tracks. The train and its passengers were carried through the air and dropped 80 feet from the tracks. There were 170 people on board. Though many people were hurt, only one person died. But in 1974, a series of tornadoes in Missouri, Illinois, Indiana, and ten other states killed 315 people in twenty-four hours.

All for the Better
by Nicholasa Mohr

The shrill whistle blared again as the ship slowly pulled away from the dock and out into San Juan Harbor. Evelina watched as first her mother and sisters and then her beautiful Island disappeared from view. Soon the soft green-blue of the Caribbean Sea and the cloudless bright sunny sky were all she was able to see.

She wondered if she would ever again see the abundant flowers and tall palm trees glistening in the bright sunshine. Would she ever again bathe in Puerto Rico's blue waters or walk along its white sandy beaches? Would she ever again bask in the warmth of her beautiful tropical Island of Puerto Rico? It was scary to think the answers to these questions might be no.

But the scariest part was being without her family. Evelina hardly remembered her Tía Vicenta, who had left Puerto Rico several years earlier. And she had never even met her aunt's new husband. She felt as if she was going to live with strangers. Evelina tried hard not to be too fearful about the future. Mami, she told herself, had done what was best for *la familia*. So she would do what she must to be brave.

Name _____ Date _____

All for the Better (continued)

Doña Clara, an acquaintance of her mother's, was also sailing on El Ponce. She had agreed to share a cabin with Evelina and to take charge of her during their voyage.

During the first day at sea, Doña Clara was very attentive. She saw to it that Evelina was safely settled in her bunk and had all she needed to be comfortable. But the following day the sea grew rough and Doña Clara became seasick. She remained sick the entire voyage and never once left their cramped little cabin.

It was Evelina who ended up taking care of Doña Clara. "You're an angel," Doña Clara whispered from her sickbed. "I'm the one who is supposed to be taking care of you." Then she insisted that Evelina mingle with the other passengers. Since Doña Clara slept most of the time, Evelina took her advice. But she always checked in on Doña Clara to make sure she was all right.

Everyone remarked on what a thoughtful and responsible girl Evelina was. Her outgoing personality and good looks endeared her to all she met. "Evelina, come have dinner with us," they would say. Or, "Evelina, join us for a game of checkers." She was always sought after, and by the time the journey was over, Evelina had made many friends on board ship.

All for the Better (continued)

To her surprise, on the last day of the voyage Evelina felt sad. Sad about leaving *El Ponce*. Sad about saying goodbye to Doña Clara and all her new friends. Everyone had been so kind! They had taken her mind away from her own sorrow. They had made the separation from her mother and sisters seem less terrible, less fearful.

But now the voyage was coming to an end. Evelina came up on deck. With all her might she wished that *El Ponce* was entering San Juan Harbor, not New York Harbor. She wanted to be back in Puerto Rico.

Evelina watched as this strange new city loomed gray and forbidding. She cringed at the sight of the tall buildings crowding across the horizon. Her heart sank as she looked around. The city skies were dreary. The water had a foul, oily smell.

A tug guided *El Ponce* to the dock. Evelina watched the workmen move around the dock shouting strange words at one another. They looped heavy ropes from the ship around the dock's iron posts. Quickly *El Ponce* was tied fast and the five-day journey was over. Doña Clara, who had recovered as soon as they had neared land again, took Evelina's hand to lead her ashore. They went down the gangplank onto the docks of South Brooklyn.

Rattlesnakes
by Russell Freedman

In rattlesnake country a dark cave in the side of a cliff might be a rattlesnake den. Rattlesnakes come to the cave when summer ends. On warm days they stretch out on the rocks and soak up the autumn sun.

As the days get colder, the snakes crawl deep inside the cave, where the frost can't reach them. They coil their bodies together into a great ball of snakes. Then they fall asleep, or hibernate, all winter long. Rattlers often share their dens with copperheads, milk snakes, garter snakes, and other kinds of snakes. Hundreds of snakes may spend the winter sleeping together in the same cave.

When spring comes, they wake up, and as the warm weather sets in, they leave their winter den for good. They crawl off in all directions, ready to prowl for food and mates.

Rattlesnakes (continued)

Rattlesnakes are found only in the Americas, especially in the United States and Mexico. They live in all sorts of wild country—in forests, prairies, and deserts; in thick underbrush and on rocky mountain slopes. There are fifteen kinds of rattlesnakes on the United States mainland. The biggest is the eastern diamondback. It can be up to eight feet long! The smallest is the scrappy little pigmy rattlesnake, which is less than two feet long.

Rattlers are pit vipers, a family of poisonous snakes that have thick bodies, narrow necks, and big, wedge-shaped heads. Pit vipers get their name from the pits in their cheeks, which they use to hunt warm-blooded animals like birds and mice. The pits sense heat. They tell the snake if an animal is nearby or how far away it is. Guided by its pits, a rattlesnake can strike at warm-blooded prey in total darkness. And it will hit its target every time.

One thing sets a rattlesnake apart from all other snakes—its rattle. When a rattler is born, it has no rattle. Instead, it has a small, hard button at the tip of its tail. The first time the young rattlesnake sheds its skin, it loses its baby-button and gains its first real rattle. From then on, a new rattle appears every time the snake sheds its skin. Each rattle is a dry, hollow scale connected loosely to the rattles on either side.

Rattlesnakes (continued)

Hearing a snake rattle in the wilderness can be very frightening. At first it sounds as if dried bones are being clicked together very rapidly. Then, as the rattler shakes its tail faster, it sounds more like the angry buzz of an insect or the hiss of escaping steam. This sound is a warning. A rattlesnake shakes its tail to scare off enemies and give itself time to escape. Its rattle can save the snake from being stepped on by a horse or attacked by a dog.

A rattlesnake's fangs are as sharp as a doctor's needle. When the fangs aren't being used, they fold back against the roof of the mouth. As the rattler opens its mouth to strike, the fangs spring forward and snap into place. A hollow tube carries poison from a gland in the rattler's cheek to a small hole at the tip of each fang.

The Girl Who Cried Flowers
by Jane Yolen

In ancient Greece, where the spirits of beautiful women were said to dwell in trees, a girl was born who cried flowers. Tears never fell from her eyes. Instead blossoms cascaded down her cheeks: scarlet, gold, and blue in the spring, and snow-white in the fall.

No one knew her real mother and father. She had been found one day wrapped in a blanket of woven grasses in the crook of an olive tree. The shepherd who found her called her Olivia after the tree and brought her home to his childless wife. Olivia lived with them as their daughter, and grew into a beautiful girl.

At first her strangeness frightened the villagers. But after a while, Olivia charmed them all with her gentle, giving nature. It was not long before the villagers were showing her off to any traveler who passed their way. For every stranger, Olivia would squeeze a tiny tear-blossom from her eyes. And that is how her fame spread throughout the land.

But soon a tiny tear-blossom was not enough. Young men wanted nosegays to give to the girls they courted. Young women wanted garlands to twine in their hair. The priests asked for bouquets to bank their altars. And old men and women begged funeral wreaths against the time of their deaths.

The Girl Who Cried Flowers (continued)

To all these requests, Olivia said yes, and so she had to spend her days thinking sad thoughts, listening to tragic tales, and crying mountains of flowers to make other people happy. Still, she did not complain, for above all things Olivia loved making other people happy—even though it made her sad.

Then one day, when she was out in her garden looking at the far mountains and trying to think of sad things to fill her mind, a young man came by. He was strong enough for two, but wise enough to ask for help when he needed it. He had heard of Olivia's magical tears and had come to beg a garland for his own proud sweetheart.

But when he saw Olivia, the thought of his proud sweetheart went entirely out of the young man's mind. He sat down by Olivia's feet and started to tell her tales, for though he was a farmer, he had the gift of telling that only true storytellers have. Soon Olivia was smiling, then laughing in delight, as the tales rolled off his tongue.

"Stop," she said at last. "I do not even know your name."

"I am called Panos," he said.

"Then, Panos, if you must tell me tales—and indeed I hope you never stop—tell me sad ones. I must fill myself with sorrow if I am to give you what you want."

"I want only you," he said, for his errand had been long forgotten. "And that is a joyous thing."

For a time it was true. Panos and Olivia were married and lived happily in a small house at the end of the village.

The Girl Who Cried Flowers (continued)

Panos worked long hours in the fields while Olivia kept their
home neat and spotless. In the evenings they laughed together
over Panos' stories or over the happenings of the day, for Panos
had forbidden Olivia ever to cry again. He said it made him
sad to see her sad. And as she wanted only to make him happy,
Olivia never let even the smallest tear come to her eyes.

But one day, an old lady waited until Panos had gone off to
the fields and then came to Olivia's house to borrow
a cup of oil.

"How goes it?" asked Olivia innocently, for since her
marriage to Panos, she had all but forsaken the villagers. And
indeed, since she would not cry flowers for them, the villagers
had forsaken her in return.

The old lady sighed. She was fine, she explained, but for
one small thing. Her granddaughter was being married in the
morning and needed a crown of blue and gold flowers. But, the
crafty old lady said, since Olivia was forbidden to cry any more
blossoms, her granddaughter would have to go to the wedding
with none.

"If only I could make her just one small crown," thought
Olivia. She became so sad at the thought that she could not
give the girl flowers without hurting Panos that tears came
unbidden to her eyes. They welled up, and as they started down
her cheeks, they turned to petals and fluttered to the floor.

The old lady quickly gathered up the blossoms and, without
a word more, left for home.

The Great Yellowstone Fire
by Carole G. Vogel and Kathryn A. Goldner

In 1988, park officials expected another normal fire season. After a dry winter, spring precipitation was high. Fires ignited by lightning all fizzled out. Then, in June, conditions changed. The air turned hot and dry, and practically no rain fell. Day after day, the sun beat down on Yellowstone. Lakes and streams shrank. In the meadows, grasses shriveled. In the forests, dead lodgepole pines and fallen branches became parched. Slowly, the landscape changed from lush green to withered brown.

Thunderstorms rumbled across the park but brought no rain. Lightning ignited many small fires. Some died quickly, while others sprang to life. The fires burned unevenly, scorching here, singeing there. They leapfrogged through the forests, leaving patches of trees and ground cover untouched. Pushed along by dry summer winds, the fires grew.

Just over the park boundary in Targhee National Forest, woodcutters accidentally started another fire. The flames quickly spread into Yellowstone. Firefighters battled this blaze and several others that threatened buildings, but they could not stop the fires.

The Great Yellowstone Fire (continued)

By midsummer, almost 9,000 acres of Yellowstone's 2.2 million acres had burned. Fires raged through forests that had taken hundreds of years to grow. No rain was expected for weeks, and officials were worried. On July 15, they decided to fight all new natural blazes. Within a week, they began to battle all existing ones, as well. Yet the fires continued to spread.

Wildfires usually burn more slowly at night, then rev up with the heat of day. But in the summer of 1988, dry night winds blew down from high ridges, fanning the blazes. Day and night, ground fires crackled through dead pine needles, branches, and logs, blackening the forest floor. In some places, they scorched the bases of trees but left the tops green. In other areas, the ground fires burned hotter and toasted needles in the crowns of the trees a dusty rust color. ...

From sunup to sunset and into the night, nearly 9,500 firefighters from all parts of the country battled the blazes. Many of these men and women prepared firebreaks. They cleared strips of ground of everything that could burn. Sometimes they scraped the land with hand tools; at other times, they detonated explosives or set small backfires. They sprayed trees and buildings with water or fire-retardant foam and snuffed out spot fires.

The Great Yellowstone Fire (continued)

To fight remote blazes, firefighters hiked into the backcountry. Smoke jumpers parachuted in. Sometimes fire crews dropped water or fire retardant onto the blazes from helicopters and airplanes. Yet the fires defied everyone's best efforts. Blazes subdued by water or retardant leapt back to life. Small fires grew and joined with bigger fires. Flames skipped over prepared firebreaks, roads, and rivers. One blaze even jumped the Grand Canyon of the Yellowstone River. By mid-August, experts agreed that only a change in weather could stop the fires.

But the forecast for hot, dry weather remained unchanged. On August 20, the day that would be called Black Saturday, gale-force winds fanned every blaze in the park. Flames rampaged through forests and meadows. Smoke billowed high into the sky, and gray ash rained down.

Powerless, firefighters could only stand and watch while fire consumed another 160,000 acres. More of Yellowstone was blackened on this one day than in the previous 116 years. The amount of burned area in the park had doubled.